50 Christmas Dinner Recipes for Home

By: Kelly Johnson

Table of Contents

- Roast Turkey with Herb Butter
- Honey Glazed Ham
- Garlic and Rosemary Prime Rib
- Stuffing with Sausage and Apples
- Classic Mashed Potatoes
- Green Bean Almondine
- Candied Yams
- Cranberry Orange Relish
- Brussels Sprouts with Bacon
- Creamy Butternut Squash Soup
- Traditional Bread Dressing
- Parmesan Garlic Roasted Potatoes
- Maple Glazed Carrots
- Spinach and Artichoke Dip
- Bacon-Wrapped Asparagus
- Sweet Potato Casserole with Marshmallows
- Herb-Crusted Beef Tenderloin
- Pecan-Crusted Chicken
- Roasted Root Vegetables
- Stuffed Acorn Squash
- Glazed Corn on the Cob
- Savory Bread Pudding
- Balsamic Roasted Brussels Sprouts
- Herb-Infused Rice Pilaf
- Creamy Spinach and Mushroom Gratin
- Garlic Butter Shrimp
- Cranberry Pecan Salad
- Roasted Red Pepper Soup
- Apple and Sausage Stuffing
- Cheddar and Chive Biscuits
- Prosciutto-Wrapped Chicken
- Roasted Beet and Goat Cheese Salad
- Brown Sugar Glazed Carrots
- Herbed Cream Cheese Mashed Potatoes
- Sweet and Sour Glazed Ham
- Butternut Squash and Sage Ravioli

- Maple-Dijon Glazed Pork Tenderloin
- Parmesan-Crusted Cauliflower
- Cranberry Stuffed Pork Loin
- Lemon-Garlic Roasted Chicken
- Spiced Apple Chutney
- Baked Macaroni and Cheese
- Winter Salad with Pomegranate Vinaigrette
- Savory Pumpkin Risotto
- Spicy Sausage and Chestnut Stuffing
- Roasted Garlic and Herb Mushrooms
- Creamy Buttermilk Mashed Potatoes
- Honey-Balsamic Roasted Carrots
- Mushroom and Gruyere Stuffed Beef Wellington
- Pear and Gorgonzola Salad

Roast Turkey with Herb Butter

Ingredients:

- 1 whole turkey (12-14 lbs), thawed
- 1 cup unsalted butter, softened
- 2 tablespoons fresh rosemary, chopped
- 2 tablespoons fresh thyme, chopped
- 2 tablespoons fresh sage, chopped
- 4 cloves garlic, minced
- 1 lemon, zested and juiced
- Salt and pepper, to taste
- 1 onion, quartered
- 1 carrot, chopped
- 1 celery stalk, chopped
- 2 cups chicken broth

Instructions:

1. **Preheat Oven**: Preheat your oven to 325°F (165°C).
2. **Prepare Herb Butter**: In a bowl, combine softened butter, rosemary, thyme, sage, garlic, lemon zest, and lemon juice. Mix well to form a herb butter.
3. **Prepare Turkey**: Remove the turkey giblets and pat the turkey dry with paper towels. Season the cavity with salt and pepper. Stuff the cavity with onion, carrot, and celery.
4. **Apply Herb Butter**: Gently loosen the skin of the turkey over the breasts by sliding your fingers between the skin and meat. Spread half of the herb butter directly onto the meat under the skin. Rub the remaining herb butter all over the outside of the turkey.
5. **Roast Turkey**: Place the turkey breast side up on a rack in a roasting pan. Pour the chicken broth into the bottom of the pan. Roast the turkey, basting occasionally with the pan juices, until a meat thermometer inserted into the thickest part of the thigh reads 165°F (74°C). This should take about 3 to 3.5 hours.
6. **Rest Turkey**: Once done, remove the turkey from the oven and let it rest for 20-30 minutes before carving. This allows the juices to redistribute throughout the meat.
7. **Serve**: Carve the turkey and serve with your favorite sides and gravy. Enjoy your flavorful, herb-infused roast turkey!

This recipe ensures a juicy and flavorful turkey, perfect for any festive occasion.

Honey Glazed Ham

Ingredients:

- 1 fully cooked bone-in ham (8-10 lbs)
- 1 cup honey
- 1/2 cup brown sugar
- 1/4 cup Dijon mustard
- 1/4 cup apple cider vinegar
- 1/4 cup orange juice
- 1/2 teaspoon ground cloves
- 1/2 teaspoon ground cinnamon
- 1/4 teaspoon black pepper
- Whole cloves (for studding the ham)

Instructions:

1. **Preheat Oven**: Preheat your oven to 325°F (165°C).
2. **Prepare Ham**: Remove the ham from its packaging and discard any plastic or netting. Place the ham, cut side down, on a rack in a roasting pan. Score the surface of the ham in a diamond pattern, making shallow cuts about 1 inch apart. Stick whole cloves into the intersections of the score marks.
3. **Make Glaze**: In a saucepan, combine honey, brown sugar, Dijon mustard, apple cider vinegar, orange juice, ground cloves, ground cinnamon, and black pepper. Cook over medium heat, stirring occasionally, until the mixture comes to a boil and the sugar is completely dissolved.
4. **Glaze Ham**: Brush the ham generously with the honey glaze, making sure to get it into the scored cuts and cloves. Reserve some glaze for basting and serving.
5. **Bake Ham**: Cover the roasting pan with aluminum foil and bake the ham for about 1.5 to 2 hours, or until heated through. Baste the ham with the reserved glaze every 30 minutes during baking.
6. **Caramelize Glaze**: In the last 20-30 minutes of baking, remove the foil and brush the ham with additional glaze. Increase the oven temperature to 400°F (200°C) and bake, uncovered, until the glaze is caramelized and bubbly.
7. **Rest and Serve**: Remove the ham from the oven and let it rest for 10-15 minutes before slicing. Serve warm, with the remaining glaze on the side.

This honey glazed ham offers a perfect blend of sweet and savory flavors, making it an ideal centerpiece for your holiday table.

Garlic and Rosemary Prime Rib

Ingredients:

- 1 bone-in prime rib roast (4-6 lbs)
- 4 cloves garlic, minced
- 2 tablespoons fresh rosemary, chopped
- 2 tablespoons olive oil
- 1 tablespoon coarse salt
- 1 tablespoon black pepper
- 1 teaspoon dried thyme
- 1 teaspoon dried rosemary
- 1 cup beef broth
- 1/2 cup red wine (optional)

Instructions:

1. **Preheat Oven**: Preheat your oven to 450°F (230°C).
2. **Prepare Prime Rib**: Pat the prime rib roast dry with paper towels. In a small bowl, mix together minced garlic, chopped rosemary, olive oil, coarse salt, black pepper, dried thyme, and dried rosemary to form a paste.
3. **Season the Roast**: Rub the garlic and rosemary paste all over the surface of the prime rib, ensuring it's well-coated. Place the roast on a rack in a roasting pan, bone side down.
4. **Roast the Meat**: Insert the roast into the preheated oven and cook at 450°F (230°C) for 15 minutes to create a seared crust. Reduce the oven temperature to 325°F (165°C) and continue roasting for about 2 to 2.5 hours, or until a meat thermometer inserted into the center reads 130°F (54°C) for medium-rare. Adjust the cooking time based on your preferred level of doneness.
5. **Rest the Roast**: Once done, remove the roast from the oven and transfer it to a cutting board. Tent loosely with aluminum foil and let it rest for 20-30 minutes to allow the juices to redistribute.
6. **Make the Au Jus**: While the roast is resting, place the roasting pan over medium heat on the stovetop. Add beef broth and red wine (if using) to the pan, scraping up any browned bits from the bottom. Bring to a simmer and reduce slightly. Strain the au jus if desired.
7. **Serve**: Slice the prime rib to your preferred thickness and serve with the au jus on the side.

This garlic and rosemary prime rib features a flavorful crust and tender, juicy meat, making it a standout dish for special occasions and holiday dinners.

Stuffing with Sausage and Apples

Ingredients:

- 1 loaf of day-old bread (about 12 cups, cubed)
- 1 pound Italian sausage (bulk, not in casings)
- 2 tablespoons unsalted butter
- 1 medium onion, diced
- 3 celery stalks, diced
- 2 apples, peeled, cored, and diced
- 2 cloves garlic, minced
- 1 teaspoon dried sage
- 1 teaspoon dried thyme
- 1/2 teaspoon dried rosemary
- 1/4 teaspoon ground black pepper
- 2 cups chicken or vegetable broth
- 1/4 cup fresh parsley, chopped (optional)

Instructions:

1. **Preheat Oven**: Preheat your oven to 350°F (175°C).
2. **Prepare Bread**: If your bread is not already stale, spread the cubed bread on a baking sheet and bake for 10-15 minutes until it's slightly dried out. Transfer to a large bowl.
3. **Cook Sausage**: In a large skillet over medium heat, cook the sausage, breaking it up with a spoon, until browned and fully cooked. Remove the sausage with a slotted spoon and set aside.
4. **Sauté Vegetables**: In the same skillet, add butter and melt over medium heat. Add diced onion, celery, and apples. Cook, stirring occasionally, until the vegetables are softened and the apples are slightly caramelized, about 8-10 minutes. Stir in minced garlic and cook for an additional 1 minute.
5. **Combine Ingredients**: Add the cooked sausage back to the skillet with the vegetables and apples. Stir in dried sage, thyme, rosemary, and black pepper. Cook for another 2 minutes to let the flavors meld together.
6. **Mix Stuffing**: Pour the sausage mixture over the cubed bread. Pour in chicken or vegetable broth gradually, stirring until the bread is evenly moistened but not soggy. If the stuffing seems too dry, add a bit more broth.
7. **Bake Stuffing**: Transfer the stuffing mixture to a greased baking dish (about 9x13 inches). Cover with aluminum foil and bake in the preheated oven for 30 minutes. Remove the foil and bake for an additional 15 minutes, or until the top is golden brown and crispy.
8. **Garnish and Serve**: If desired, sprinkle with fresh parsley before serving.

This stuffing with sausage and apples combines savory sausage with sweet, crisp apples, creating a delightful side dish that complements any holiday or festive meal.

Classic Mashed Potatoes

Ingredients:

- 2 pounds Yukon Gold or Russet potatoes, peeled and cut into chunks
- 1/2 cup unsalted butter (1 stick), cubed
- 1 cup whole milk (or heavy cream for richer potatoes)
- 1/4 cup sour cream (optional for extra creaminess)
- 2 cloves garlic, minced (optional)
- Salt and freshly ground black pepper, to taste
- Chives or parsley, chopped (for garnish, optional)

Instructions:

1. **Cook Potatoes**: Place the peeled and chunked potatoes in a large pot and cover with cold water. Add a generous pinch of salt. Bring to a boil over high heat, then reduce heat to medium and simmer until the potatoes are tender when pierced with a fork, about 15-20 minutes.
2. **Drain and Dry**: Drain the potatoes in a colander and let them sit for a few minutes to steam dry. This helps to remove excess moisture, making for fluffier mashed potatoes.
3. **Mash Potatoes**: Return the potatoes to the pot or a large mixing bowl. Use a potato masher to begin mashing the potatoes. For extra smooth potatoes, you can use a potato ricer or food mill.
4. **Add Butter and Cream**: While the potatoes are still warm, add the cubed butter and stir until melted and incorporated. Gradually add the warm milk (or cream), mixing until the potatoes reach your desired consistency. If using sour cream, fold it in at this stage.
5. **Season and Adjust**: Season with salt and freshly ground black pepper to taste. If you're using garlic, stir it in now.
6. **Serve**: Transfer the mashed potatoes to a serving dish. Garnish with chopped chives or parsley, if desired.

This classic mashed potatoes recipe offers a creamy, buttery side dish that pairs beautifully with roast meats, gravies, and holiday fare.

Green Bean Almondine

Ingredients:

- 1 pound fresh green beans, trimmed
- 3 tablespoons unsalted butter
- 1/2 cup sliced almonds
- 2 cloves garlic, minced
- 1 lemon, zested and juiced
- Salt and freshly ground black pepper, to taste
- 1 tablespoon fresh parsley, chopped (for garnish, optional)

Instructions:

1. **Blanch Green Beans**: Bring a large pot of salted water to a boil. Add the green beans and cook for 3-4 minutes, or until tender-crisp. Drain and immediately plunge the green beans into a bowl of ice water to stop the cooking process and preserve the bright green color. Drain again and set aside.
2. **Toast Almonds**: In a large skillet, melt the butter over medium heat. Add the sliced almonds and cook, stirring frequently, until they are golden brown and fragrant, about 3-4 minutes. Be careful not to burn them.
3. **Sauté Garlic**: Add the minced garlic to the skillet and cook for an additional 1 minute, until fragrant.
4. **Add Green Beans**: Add the blanched green beans to the skillet and toss to coat them with the butter and almonds. Cook for 2-3 minutes, or until the green beans are heated through.
5. **Season and Finish**: Remove from heat and stir in the lemon zest and lemon juice. Season with salt and freshly ground black pepper to taste.
6. **Garnish and Serve**: Transfer the green beans to a serving dish and garnish with fresh parsley if desired.

Green Bean Almondine offers a delightful combination of crisp green beans, toasted almonds, and a hint of lemon, making it a perfect side dish for both everyday meals and special occasions.

Candied Yams

Ingredients:

- 4 large yams or sweet potatoes, peeled and cut into 1-inch cubes
- 1/2 cup unsalted butter
- 1 cup brown sugar, packed
- 1/2 cup pure maple syrup or light corn syrup
- 1/2 teaspoon ground cinnamon
- 1/4 teaspoon ground nutmeg
- 1/4 teaspoon salt
- 1/2 cup pecans or walnuts, chopped (optional)
- 1/4 cup mini marshmallows (optional)

Instructions:

1. **Preheat Oven**: Preheat your oven to 375°F (190°C).
2. **Boil Yams**: Place the yam cubes in a large pot and cover with water. Bring to a boil and cook for about 10 minutes, or until just tender. Drain and set aside.
3. **Prepare Sauce**: In a medium saucepan, melt the butter over medium heat. Stir in the brown sugar, maple syrup (or corn syrup), cinnamon, nutmeg, and salt. Cook, stirring frequently, until the mixture is smooth and the sugar has dissolved.
4. **Combine and Bake**: In a large mixing bowl, toss the cooked yam cubes with the brown sugar mixture until evenly coated. Transfer the yams and sauce to a greased baking dish.
5. **Add Nuts (Optional)**: If using, sprinkle chopped pecans or walnuts over the top of the yams.
6. **Bake**: Cover the baking dish with aluminum foil and bake in the preheated oven for 20-25 minutes, or until the yams are tender and the sauce is bubbly. Remove the foil during the last 10 minutes of baking.
7. **Add Marshmallows (Optional)**: If using mini marshmallows, sprinkle them over the yams during the last 5 minutes of baking. Return to the oven until the marshmallows are golden brown and slightly melted.
8. **Serve**: Let the candied yams cool slightly before serving.

Candied yams are a sweet and comforting side dish, perfect for holiday dinners or special occasions. The combination of tender yams with a rich, sugary glaze creates a dish that's both indulgent and delicious.

Cranberry Orange Relish

Ingredients:

- 12 ounces fresh cranberries (about 3 cups)
- 1 large orange, peeled and sectioned
- 1 cup granulated sugar
- 1/2 cup water
- 1/2 teaspoon ground cinnamon (optional)
- 1/4 teaspoon ground cloves (optional)
- 1/4 cup chopped pecans or walnuts (optional)

Instructions:

1. **Prepare Ingredients**: Rinse the cranberries and discard any that are soft or damaged. Peel the orange and separate it into sections, removing any seeds.
2. **Process Fruit**: In a food processor, combine the cranberries and orange sections. Pulse until the mixture is finely chopped but still chunky. You may need to do this in batches depending on the size of your food processor.
3. **Cook Relish**: In a medium saucepan, combine the chopped cranberry-orange mixture with sugar and water. Stir to combine. If using, add ground cinnamon and cloves. Bring the mixture to a boil over medium heat, stirring frequently.
4. **Simmer**: Reduce the heat to low and simmer for 10-15 minutes, or until the cranberries burst and the relish thickens slightly. Stir occasionally to prevent sticking.
5. **Cool and Add Nuts**: Remove from heat and let the relish cool to room temperature. If desired, stir in the chopped pecans or walnuts once cooled.
6. **Serve**: Transfer the cranberry orange relish to a serving dish or store in an airtight container in the refrigerator until ready to serve.

Cranberry Orange Relish is a vibrant, tangy condiment that adds a fresh and zesty touch to your holiday meals. Its combination of tart cranberries and sweet orange makes it a perfect complement to roast meats and festive dishes.

Brussels Sprouts with Bacon

Ingredients:

- 1 pound Brussels sprouts, trimmed and halved
- 4 slices bacon, chopped
- 1 medium onion, finely diced
- 2 cloves garlic, minced
- 1 tablespoon olive oil
- Salt and freshly ground black pepper, to taste
- 1/4 cup balsamic vinegar (optional)
- 1/4 cup grated Parmesan cheese (optional)
- 1 tablespoon fresh parsley, chopped (for garnish, optional)

Instructions:

1. **Prepare Brussels Sprouts**: Trim the ends of the Brussels sprouts and cut them in half. Set aside.
2. **Cook Bacon**: In a large skillet or sauté pan, cook the chopped bacon over medium heat until crispy, about 6-8 minutes. Use a slotted spoon to remove the bacon from the pan and set it aside on a paper towel-lined plate. Leave the bacon drippings in the pan.
3. **Sauté Vegetables**: Add the diced onion to the skillet with the bacon drippings and cook over medium heat until softened, about 5 minutes. Add the minced garlic and cook for an additional 1 minute, stirring frequently.
4. **Cook Brussels Sprouts**: Add the halved Brussels sprouts to the skillet, tossing to coat them with the bacon drippings and onions. Cook, stirring occasionally, for about 10-12 minutes, or until the Brussels sprouts are tender and caramelized. If necessary, add a tablespoon of olive oil if the pan is too dry.
5. **Season and Finish**: Season with salt and freshly ground black pepper to taste. If using, drizzle with balsamic vinegar and cook for an additional 1-2 minutes, allowing the vinegar to reduce slightly and glaze the sprouts.
6. **Add Bacon**: Stir the crispy bacon pieces back into the Brussels sprouts.
7. **Garnish and Serve**: Transfer the Brussels sprouts to a serving dish. If desired, sprinkle with grated Parmesan cheese and chopped fresh parsley.

Brussels Sprouts with Bacon offers a savory and satisfying side dish with the perfect balance of crispy bacon and tender, caramelized sprouts. The optional balsamic vinegar adds a touch of sweetness and tang, enhancing the flavors of this classic favorite.

Creamy Butternut Squash Soup

Ingredients:

- 1 medium butternut squash (about 2 pounds), peeled, seeded, and cubed
- 2 tablespoons olive oil
- 1 medium onion, diced
- 2 cloves garlic, minced
- 1 large carrot, peeled and diced
- 2 celery stalks, diced
- 1 teaspoon ground cumin
- 1/2 teaspoon ground cinnamon
- 1/4 teaspoon ground nutmeg
- 4 cups vegetable or chicken broth
- 1 cup coconut milk or heavy cream
- Salt and freshly ground black pepper, to taste
- 1 tablespoon fresh parsley or chives, chopped (for garnish, optional)
- 1 tablespoon maple syrup or honey (optional, for added sweetness)

Instructions:

1. **Preheat Oven**: Preheat your oven to 400°F (200°C).
2. **Roast Squash**: Toss the cubed butternut squash with 1 tablespoon of olive oil, salt, and pepper. Spread the squash in a single layer on a baking sheet. Roast in the preheated oven for 25-30 minutes, or until tender and caramelized, turning once halfway through cooking.
3. **Sauté Vegetables**: While the squash is roasting, heat the remaining 1 tablespoon of olive oil in a large pot over medium heat. Add the diced onion, carrot, and celery. Cook, stirring occasionally, until the vegetables are softened, about 8-10 minutes. Add the minced garlic, cumin, cinnamon, and nutmeg, and cook for an additional 1-2 minutes, until fragrant.
4. **Combine Ingredients**: Once the squash is roasted, add it to the pot with the sautéed vegetables. Pour in the vegetable or chicken broth and bring to a boil. Reduce the heat and simmer for 10 minutes to let the flavors meld.
5. **Blend Soup**: Use an immersion blender to puree the soup until smooth. Alternatively, carefully transfer the soup in batches to a blender and blend until smooth. Return the pureed soup to the pot.
6. **Add Cream**: Stir in the coconut milk or heavy cream. Heat the soup over low heat until warmed through. Adjust seasoning with salt, pepper, and maple syrup or honey if desired.
7. **Garnish and Serve**: Ladle the soup into bowls and garnish with fresh parsley or chives if desired.

This creamy butternut squash soup is rich and velvety, offering a comforting blend of sweet, savory, and warm spices. It's perfect for a cozy lunch or dinner, especially during the cooler months.

Traditional Bread Dressing

Ingredients:

- 1 loaf of day-old bread (about 12 cups, cubed; preferably a mix of white and whole wheat)
- 1/2 cup unsalted butter
- 1 large onion, finely diced
- 3 celery stalks, finely diced
- 2 cloves garlic, minced
- 1 tablespoon fresh sage, chopped (or 1 teaspoon dried sage)
- 1 tablespoon fresh thyme, chopped (or 1 teaspoon dried thyme)
- 1 teaspoon dried rosemary
- 1/2 teaspoon ground black pepper
- 1/2 teaspoon salt (or to taste)
- 2-3 cups chicken or vegetable broth (more as needed)
- 2 large eggs, beaten
- 1/4 cup fresh parsley, chopped (optional)

Instructions:

1. **Preheat Oven**: Preheat your oven to 350°F (175°C).
2. **Prepare Bread**: If the bread is not already stale, spread the cubed bread on a baking sheet and toast in the oven for about 10-15 minutes, until slightly dried out. Transfer to a large mixing bowl.
3. **Sauté Vegetables**: In a large skillet, melt the butter over medium heat. Add the diced onion and celery, and cook until softened, about 8-10 minutes. Add the minced garlic and cook for an additional 1 minute. Stir in the fresh sage, thyme, rosemary, black pepper, and salt.
4. **Combine Ingredients**: Pour the sautéed vegetables and herbs over the bread cubes in the mixing bowl. Toss to combine evenly.
5. **Add Broth and Eggs**: Gradually add chicken or vegetable broth, tossing the bread mixture to evenly moisten the bread. You may need more or less broth depending on the dryness of the bread. The mixture should be slightly moist but not soggy. Stir in the beaten eggs and mix until well combined.
6. **Bake Dressing**: Transfer the dressing mixture to a greased baking dish (about 9x13 inches). Cover with aluminum foil and bake for 30 minutes. Remove the foil and bake for an additional 15-20 minutes, or until the top is golden brown and crisp.
7. **Garnish and Serve**: If desired, garnish with chopped fresh parsley before serving.

This traditional bread dressing is a classic side dish that's perfect for holiday meals and special gatherings. It's savory, flavorful, and complements roasted meats and gravies beautifully.

Parmesan Garlic Roasted Potatoes

Ingredients:

- 1.5 pounds baby potatoes or small Yukon Gold potatoes, halved or quartered
- 3 tablespoons olive oil
- 4 cloves garlic, minced
- 1/2 cup grated Parmesan cheese
- 1 teaspoon dried oregano
- 1/2 teaspoon dried rosemary
- 1/2 teaspoon paprika
- Salt and freshly ground black pepper, to taste
- 2 tablespoons fresh parsley, chopped (for garnish, optional)

Instructions:

1. **Preheat Oven**: Preheat your oven to 425°F (220°C).
2. **Prepare Potatoes**: Wash and cut the potatoes into uniform pieces to ensure even cooking. Pat them dry with paper towels.
3. **Season Potatoes**: In a large bowl, toss the potato pieces with olive oil, minced garlic, Parmesan cheese, dried oregano, dried rosemary, paprika, salt, and black pepper until evenly coated.
4. **Arrange and Roast**: Spread the seasoned potatoes in a single layer on a baking sheet. Avoid overcrowding the pan to ensure crispy results.
5. **Bake Potatoes**: Roast in the preheated oven for 25-30 minutes, or until the potatoes are golden brown and crispy on the outside, and tender inside. Toss the potatoes halfway through cooking for even browning.
6. **Garnish and Serve**: Remove from the oven and garnish with chopped fresh parsley if desired. Serve warm.

These Parmesan Garlic Roasted Potatoes are a delicious and crispy side dish, perfect for complementing a wide range of main courses. The combination of garlic and Parmesan adds a savory richness that elevates these roasted potatoes to a new level.

Maple Glazed Carrots

Ingredients:

- 1 pound carrots, peeled and cut into bite-sized pieces
- 2 tablespoons unsalted butter
- 1/4 cup pure maple syrup
- 2 tablespoons brown sugar
- 1/2 teaspoon ground cinnamon
- 1/4 teaspoon ground nutmeg
- Salt and freshly ground black pepper, to taste
- 1 tablespoon fresh parsley or chives, chopped (for garnish, optional)

Instructions:

1. **Prepare Carrots**: Peel and cut the carrots into bite-sized pieces or rounds.
2. **Cook Carrots**: In a large pot, bring water to a boil. Add the carrots and a pinch of salt. Cook until the carrots are tender but still crisp, about 5-7 minutes. Drain and set aside.
3. **Make Maple Glaze**: In a large skillet, melt the butter over medium heat. Add the maple syrup, brown sugar, ground cinnamon, and ground nutmeg. Stir to combine and bring to a simmer.
4. **Glaze Carrots**: Add the cooked carrots to the skillet and toss to coat with the maple glaze. Cook for an additional 5-7 minutes, stirring occasionally, until the carrots are well-coated and the glaze has thickened slightly.
5. **Season and Serve**: Season with salt and freshly ground black pepper to taste. Garnish with chopped fresh parsley or chives if desired.

These Maple Glazed Carrots are a sweet and savory side dish that pairs perfectly with a variety of main courses. The combination of maple syrup and brown sugar creates a delicious glaze that enhances the natural sweetness of the carrots.

Spinach and Artichoke Dip

Ingredients:

- 1 tablespoon olive oil
- 1 small onion, finely diced
- 2 cloves garlic, minced
- 1 cup frozen spinach, thawed and squeezed dry
- 1 cup canned artichoke hearts, drained and chopped
- 1 cup sour cream
- 1 cup mayonnaise
- 1 cup grated Parmesan cheese
- 1 cup shredded mozzarella cheese
- 1/4 teaspoon crushed red pepper flakes (optional, for a bit of heat)
- Salt and freshly ground black pepper, to taste
- 1/4 cup fresh parsley or basil, chopped (for garnish, optional)

Instructions:

1. **Preheat Oven**: Preheat your oven to 375°F (190°C).
2. **Sauté Vegetables**: In a medium skillet, heat olive oil over medium heat. Add the diced onion and cook until softened and translucent, about 5 minutes. Add the minced garlic and cook for an additional 1 minute, until fragrant.
3. **Combine Ingredients**: In a large bowl, mix together the sautéed onion and garlic with the thawed spinach, chopped artichoke hearts, sour cream, mayonnaise, Parmesan cheese, mozzarella cheese, and crushed red pepper flakes (if using). Season with salt and freshly ground black pepper to taste.
4. **Bake Dip**: Transfer the mixture to a baking dish (about 8x8 inches) and spread it out evenly. Bake in the preheated oven for 25-30 minutes, or until the dip is hot, bubbly, and the top is golden brown.
5. **Garnish and Serve**: Remove from the oven and let cool slightly before serving. Garnish with chopped fresh parsley or basil if desired.

Serve this Spinach and Artichoke Dip with tortilla chips, pita bread, crackers, or fresh vegetable sticks. It's a creamy, cheesy appetizer that's always a hit at parties and gatherings!

Bacon-Wrapped Asparagus

Ingredients:

- 1 bunch of asparagus (about 1 pound), trimmed
- 8-10 slices of bacon
- 1 tablespoon olive oil
- 1/4 teaspoon garlic powder
- 1/4 teaspoon onion powder
- Salt and freshly ground black pepper, to taste
- 1 tablespoon fresh lemon juice (optional, for finishing)
- 1 tablespoon fresh parsley, chopped (for garnish, optional)

Instructions:

1. **Preheat Oven**: Preheat your oven to 400°F (200°C).
2. **Prepare Asparagus**: Wash and trim the asparagus, removing the tough ends.
3. **Wrap Asparagus**: Wrap 3-4 asparagus spears with one slice of bacon, starting at the bottom and spiraling up to the tip. Secure with toothpicks if needed. Repeat with the remaining asparagus and bacon.
4. **Season**: Place the bacon-wrapped asparagus on a baking sheet. Drizzle with olive oil and sprinkle with garlic powder, onion powder, salt, and black pepper.
5. **Bake**: Bake in the preheated oven for 20-25 minutes, or until the bacon is crispy and the asparagus is tender. If desired, broil for an additional 2-3 minutes to crisp up the bacon further, keeping a close eye to prevent burning.
6. **Finish and Serve**: Remove from the oven and let cool slightly. If desired, drizzle with fresh lemon juice and garnish with chopped parsley before serving.

These Bacon-Wrapped Asparagus bundles are a savory and flavorful appetizer or side dish that combines the crispness of asparagus with the rich taste of bacon. They're perfect for both casual meals and special occasions.

Sweet Potato Casserole with Marshmallows

Ingredients:

- 4 cups cooked and mashed sweet potatoes (about 3-4 large sweet potatoes)
- 1/2 cup granulated sugar
- 1/4 cup packed brown sugar
- 1/2 cup unsalted butter, softened
- 2 large eggs
- 1/2 cup milk (whole milk or heavy cream)
- 1 teaspoon vanilla extract
- 1/2 teaspoon ground cinnamon
- 1/4 teaspoon ground nutmeg
- 1/4 teaspoon salt
- 2 cups mini marshmallows (or more, if desired)

Instructions:

1. **Preheat Oven**: Preheat your oven to 350°F (175°C).
2. **Prepare Sweet Potatoes**: If you haven't already, peel and cube the sweet potatoes. Boil or bake them until tender, then mash until smooth. You should have about 4 cups of mashed sweet potatoes.
3. **Mix Casserole Base**: In a large bowl, combine the mashed sweet potatoes with granulated sugar, brown sugar, softened butter, eggs, milk, vanilla extract, ground cinnamon, ground nutmeg, and salt. Mix until well combined and smooth.
4. **Transfer to Baking Dish**: Spoon the sweet potato mixture into a greased 9x13-inch baking dish or similar-sized dish, spreading it evenly.
5. **Bake Casserole**: Bake in the preheated oven for 25 minutes, or until the casserole is set and slightly firm.
6. **Add Marshmallows**: Remove the casserole from the oven and evenly sprinkle the mini marshmallows over the top.
7. **Finish Baking**: Return the casserole to the oven and bake for an additional 10-15 minutes, or until the marshmallows are golden brown and slightly melted.
8. **Serve**: Allow the casserole to cool slightly before serving.

This Sweet Potato Casserole with Marshmallows is a classic holiday favorite that pairs sweet, creamy mashed sweet potatoes with a gooey marshmallow topping. It's perfect as a comforting side dish for festive meals.

Herb-Crusted Beef Tenderloin

Ingredients:

- 1 (2.5 to 3 pounds) beef tenderloin, trimmed
- 2 tablespoons olive oil
- 2 tablespoons Dijon mustard
- 3 cloves garlic, minced
- 2 tablespoons fresh rosemary, chopped (or 2 teaspoons dried rosemary)
- 2 tablespoons fresh thyme, chopped (or 2 teaspoons dried thyme)
- 1 tablespoon fresh parsley, chopped (optional, for extra flavor)
- 1 tablespoon coarse salt
- 1 teaspoon ground black pepper

Instructions:

1. **Preheat Oven**: Preheat your oven to 400°F (200°C).
2. **Prepare Tenderloin**: Pat the beef tenderloin dry with paper towels. Season the meat with salt and black pepper on all sides.
3. **Sear Tenderloin**: Heat olive oil in a large, ovenproof skillet over medium-high heat. Once the oil is hot, sear the beef tenderloin for 2-3 minutes on each side, or until it develops a brown crust. Remove from heat.
4. **Prepare Herb Mixture**: In a small bowl, combine Dijon mustard, minced garlic, chopped rosemary, chopped thyme, and chopped parsley (if using). Stir to form a paste.
5. **Apply Herb Crust**: Brush the seared tenderloin with the herb paste, coating it evenly on all sides.
6. **Roast Tenderloin**: Transfer the skillet with the tenderloin to the preheated oven. Roast for 25-30 minutes, or until the internal temperature reaches 130°F (54°C) for medium-rare, or 140°F (60°C) for medium. Use a meat thermometer for accuracy.
7. **Rest and Slice**: Remove the tenderloin from the oven and let it rest for 10-15 minutes before slicing. This allows the juices to redistribute and the meat to finish cooking.
8. **Serve**: Slice the tenderloin into medallions and serve with your favorite sides.

This Herb-Crusted Beef Tenderloin is a flavorful and elegant dish, perfect for special occasions or holiday dinners. The combination of fresh herbs and Dijon mustard creates a savory crust that enhances the tender, juicy beef.

Pecan-Crusted Chicken

Ingredients:

- 4 boneless, skinless chicken breasts
- 1 cup pecans, finely chopped
- 1/2 cup panko breadcrumbs (or regular breadcrumbs)
- 1/4 cup grated Parmesan cheese
- 1/2 teaspoon garlic powder
- 1/2 teaspoon onion powder
- 1/2 teaspoon paprika
- 1/2 teaspoon dried thyme
- Salt and freshly ground black pepper, to taste
- 2 large eggs
- 1/4 cup all-purpose flour
- 2 tablespoons olive oil (for frying) or cooking spray (for baking)

Instructions:

1. **Preheat Oven (if baking)**: Preheat your oven to 375°F (190°C). Line a baking sheet with parchment paper or lightly grease it with cooking spray.
2. **Prepare Breading Station**: Set up a breading station with three shallow dishes:
   - In the first dish, place the all-purpose flour.
   - In the second dish, beat the eggs.
   - In the third dish, combine the finely chopped pecans, panko breadcrumbs, Parmesan cheese, garlic powder, onion powder, paprika, dried thyme, salt, and pepper.
3. **Coat Chicken**: Season the chicken breasts with salt and pepper. Dredge each chicken breast in the flour, shaking off excess. Dip it into the beaten eggs, then press it into the pecan mixture, coating it evenly.
4. **Cook Chicken**:
   - **For Baking**: Place the coated chicken breasts on the prepared baking sheet. Lightly brush or spray the tops with olive oil. Bake in the preheated oven for 25-30 minutes, or until the chicken is cooked through and the crust is golden brown and crispy. The internal temperature should reach 165°F (74°C).
   - **For Frying**: Heat olive oil in a large skillet over medium heat. Add the coated chicken breasts and cook for 4-5 minutes per side, or until the chicken is cooked through and the crust is golden brown and crispy. The internal temperature should reach 165°F (74°C). Remove from the skillet and drain on paper towels.
5. **Serve**: Let the chicken rest for a few minutes before slicing. Serve with your favorite sides or a light salad.

Pecan-Crusted Chicken offers a delightful crunch and nutty flavor thanks to the pecan crust. It's a delicious alternative to traditional breaded chicken and pairs well with a variety of vegetables and sauces.

Roasted Root Vegetables

Ingredients:

- 4 medium carrots, peeled and cut into 1-inch pieces
- 2 medium parsnips, peeled and cut into 1-inch pieces
- 1 medium sweet potato, peeled and cut into 1-inch pieces
- 1 medium red or yellow potato, peeled and cut into 1-inch pieces
- 1 small red onion, cut into wedges
- 3 tablespoons olive oil
- 2 teaspoons fresh rosemary, chopped (or 1 teaspoon dried rosemary)
- 2 teaspoons fresh thyme, chopped (or 1 teaspoon dried thyme)
- 1 teaspoon garlic powder
- 1 teaspoon onion powder
- Salt and freshly ground black pepper, to taste
- 1 tablespoon balsamic vinegar (optional, for added flavor)
- 1 tablespoon fresh parsley, chopped (for garnish, optional)

Instructions:

1. **Preheat Oven**: Preheat your oven to 425°F (220°C). Line a large baking sheet with parchment paper or lightly grease it.
2. **Prepare Vegetables**: Wash, peel, and cut the vegetables into 1-inch pieces. Try to keep the pieces roughly the same size to ensure even cooking.
3. **Season Vegetables**: In a large bowl, toss the cut vegetables with olive oil, rosemary, thyme, garlic powder, onion powder, salt, and black pepper until evenly coated.
4. **Arrange and Roast**: Spread the seasoned vegetables in a single layer on the prepared baking sheet. Avoid overcrowding the pan to allow for even roasting.
5. **Bake**: Roast in the preheated oven for 25-35 minutes, or until the vegetables are tender and golden brown, stirring once halfway through for even cooking. The exact time may vary depending on the size and type of vegetables used.
6. **Finish with Balsamic Vinegar (Optional)**: If desired, drizzle with balsamic vinegar during the last 5 minutes of roasting for a touch of sweetness and tang.
7. **Garnish and Serve**: Remove the vegetables from the oven and transfer to a serving dish. Garnish with chopped fresh parsley if desired.

These Roasted Root Vegetables are a versatile and hearty side dish, perfect for complementing a variety of main courses. The blend of herbs and spices enhances their natural sweetness, making them a flavorful and comforting addition to any meal.

Stuffed Acorn Squash

Ingredients:

- 2 medium acorn squash
- 1 tablespoon olive oil
- 1/2 cup onion, finely diced
- 2 cloves garlic, minced
- 1 cup cooked quinoa or rice
- 1/2 cup dried cranberries
- 1/2 cup chopped pecans or walnuts
- 1/2 cup shredded cheese (such as Gruyère, cheddar, or feta)
- 1/4 cup fresh parsley, chopped (plus extra for garnish)
- 1/2 teaspoon dried thyme
- 1/2 teaspoon dried rosemary
- 1/4 teaspoon ground cinnamon
- Salt and freshly ground black pepper, to taste
- 2 tablespoons maple syrup (optional, for drizzling)

Instructions:

1. **Preheat Oven**: Preheat your oven to 400°F (200°C).
2. **Prepare Squash**: Cut the acorn squash in half from stem to base and scoop out the seeds and stringy bits. Place the squash halves cut-side up on a baking sheet. Brush the insides with olive oil and season with salt and pepper.
3. **Roast Squash**: Roast in the preheated oven for 25-30 minutes, or until the flesh is tender and slightly caramelized.
4. **Prepare Filling**: While the squash is roasting, heat olive oil in a skillet over medium heat. Add the diced onion and cook until softened, about 5 minutes. Add the minced garlic and cook for an additional 1 minute, until fragrant.
5. **Combine Ingredients**: In a large bowl, combine the cooked quinoa or rice, sautéed onion and garlic, dried cranberries, chopped pecans or walnuts, shredded cheese, chopped parsley, dried thyme, dried rosemary, ground cinnamon, salt, and black pepper. Mix until well combined.
6. **Stuff Squash**: Once the squash is roasted and tender, remove from the oven. Spoon the filling evenly into each squash half, packing it in slightly.
7. **Bake Again**: Return the stuffed squash to the oven and bake for an additional 10-15 minutes, or until the filling is heated through and the cheese is melted and bubbly.
8. **Finish and Serve**: If desired, drizzle with maple syrup before serving. Garnish with additional chopped parsley.

Stuffed Acorn Squash is a delightful and festive dish that combines the sweetness of the squash with a savory and satisfying filling. It's perfect for holiday meals or as a hearty vegetarian main course.

Glazed Corn on the Cob

Ingredients:

- 6 ears of corn, husked and cleaned
- 4 tablespoons unsalted butter, melted
- 1/4 cup honey or maple syrup
- 2 tablespoons brown sugar
- 1/2 teaspoon ground cinnamon
- 1/4 teaspoon ground nutmeg
- 1/4 teaspoon smoked paprika (optional, for a smoky flavor)
- Salt, to taste
- Freshly ground black pepper, to taste
- Fresh parsley or chives, chopped (for garnish, optional)

Instructions:

1. **Prepare Corn**: Husk the corn and remove all the silk. Break the ears in half if they are too large for your cooking method.
2. **Cook Corn**:
    - **Boiling Method**: In a large pot of boiling salted water, cook the corn for 5-7 minutes, or until tender. Drain and set aside.
    - **Grilling Method**: Preheat the grill to medium-high heat. Place the corn on the grill and cook, turning occasionally, for 10-12 minutes, or until tender and slightly charred. Remove from the grill and set aside.
3. **Prepare Glaze**: In a small bowl, whisk together the melted butter, honey or maple syrup, brown sugar, ground cinnamon, ground nutmeg, and smoked paprika (if using).
4. **Glaze Corn**: Brush the cooked corn with the glaze mixture, making sure to coat all sides evenly. For extra flavor, you can reserve some of the glaze to brush on after serving.
5. **Serve**: Season with salt and freshly ground black pepper to taste. Garnish with chopped fresh parsley or chives if desired.

This Glazed Corn on the Cob is a sweet and savory treat that's perfect for summer barbecues, holiday meals, or as a delicious side dish any time of year. The combination of honey or maple syrup with butter and spices creates a delightful glaze that enhances the natural sweetness of the corn.

Savory Bread Pudding

Ingredients:

- 1 loaf of day-old bread (about 12 cups, cubed; preferably a mix of white and whole wheat)
- 4 tablespoons unsalted butter, divided
- 1 medium onion, finely diced
- 2 cloves garlic, minced
- 2 cups fresh spinach, chopped (or 1 cup frozen spinach, thawed and drained)
- 1 cup cooked sausage or bacon, crumbled (optional)
- 1 cup shredded cheese (such as cheddar, Gruyère, or a mix)
- 4 large eggs
- 2 cups milk (whole milk or half-and-half)
- 1/2 cup chicken or vegetable broth
- 1 tablespoon fresh thyme, chopped (or 1 teaspoon dried thyme)
- 1 tablespoon fresh parsley, chopped (for garnish, optional)
- Salt and freshly ground black pepper, to taste

Instructions:

1. **Preheat Oven**: Preheat your oven to 350°F (175°C). Grease a 9x13-inch baking dish or similar-sized dish with butter or cooking spray.
2. **Prepare Bread**: If the bread is not already stale, spread the cubed bread on a baking sheet and toast in the oven for about 10-15 minutes, until slightly dried out. Transfer to a large mixing bowl.
3. **Sauté Vegetables**: In a large skillet, melt 2 tablespoons of butter over medium heat. Add the diced onion and cook until softened, about 5-7 minutes. Add the minced garlic and cook for an additional 1 minute, until fragrant. Stir in the spinach and cook until wilted. Remove from heat and let cool slightly.
4. **Combine Ingredients**: Add the sautéed vegetables, crumbled sausage or bacon (if using), and shredded cheese to the bowl with the toasted bread. Toss to combine.
5. **Prepare Custard**: In a separate bowl, whisk together the eggs, milk, chicken or vegetable broth, fresh thyme, salt, and black pepper.
6. **Assemble Pudding**: Pour the egg mixture over the bread mixture, gently tossing to ensure all the bread cubes are evenly coated. Let the mixture sit for 10-15 minutes to allow the bread to soak up the custard.
7. **Bake**: Transfer the mixture to the prepared baking dish. Dot the top with the remaining 2 tablespoons of butter, cut into small pieces. Bake in the preheated oven for 35-45 minutes, or until the pudding is set and the top is golden brown.
8. **Garnish and Serve**: Remove from the oven and let cool slightly before serving. Garnish with chopped fresh parsley if desired.

Savory Bread Pudding is a versatile and comforting dish that can be served as a side or a main course. The combination of bread, cheese, and vegetables creates a rich, hearty pudding that's perfect for breakfast, brunch, or dinner.

Balsamic Roasted Brussels Sprouts

Ingredients:

- 1.5 pounds Brussels sprouts, trimmed and halved
- 3 tablespoons olive oil
- 3 tablespoons balsamic vinegar
- 2 tablespoons honey or maple syrup
- 3 cloves garlic, minced
- 1/2 teaspoon dried thyme (or 1 teaspoon fresh thyme)
- 1/2 teaspoon dried rosemary (or 1 teaspoon fresh rosemary)
- Salt and freshly ground black pepper, to taste
- 1/4 cup shaved Parmesan cheese (optional, for garnish)
- 1/4 cup chopped walnuts or pecans (optional, for garnish)

Instructions:

1. **Preheat Oven**: Preheat your oven to 425°F (220°C). Line a baking sheet with parchment paper or lightly grease it.
2. **Prepare Brussels Sprouts**: Trim the ends off the Brussels sprouts and cut them in half lengthwise. Place them in a large bowl.
3. **Make Balsamic Glaze**: In a small bowl, whisk together olive oil, balsamic vinegar, honey or maple syrup, minced garlic, dried thyme, dried rosemary, salt, and black pepper.
4. **Toss and Coat**: Pour the balsamic glaze over the Brussels sprouts and toss to coat evenly.
5. **Roast**: Spread the Brussels sprouts in a single layer on the prepared baking sheet. Avoid overcrowding to ensure they roast evenly.
6. **Bake**: Roast in the preheated oven for 20-25 minutes, or until the Brussels sprouts are tender and caramelized, stirring halfway through cooking.
7. **Finish and Serve**: Remove from the oven and, if desired, sprinkle with shaved Parmesan cheese and chopped nuts for added texture and flavor. Serve warm.

These Balsamic Roasted Brussels Sprouts offer a delicious blend of tangy balsamic glaze and sweet honey, creating a caramelized and flavorful side dish that pairs perfectly with a variety of main courses.

Herb-Infused Rice Pilaf

Ingredients:

- 1 cup long-grain rice (such as basmati or jasmine)
- 2 tablespoons unsalted butter or olive oil
- 1 small onion, finely diced
- 2 cloves garlic, minced
- 1/4 cup dry white wine (optional)
- 2 cups chicken or vegetable broth
- 1/2 teaspoon dried thyme
- 1/2 teaspoon dried rosemary
- 1/4 cup fresh parsley, chopped
- 1/4 cup fresh chives, chopped (optional)
- Salt and freshly ground black pepper, to taste
- 1/4 cup slivered almonds or pine nuts (optional, for garnish)

Instructions:

1. **Rinse Rice**: Rinse the rice under cold water until the water runs clear. This helps remove excess starch and prevents the rice from being too sticky.
2. **Sauté Aromatics**: In a medium saucepan, melt the butter or heat the olive oil over medium heat. Add the diced onion and cook until softened and translucent, about 5 minutes. Add the minced garlic and cook for an additional 1 minute.
3. **Toast Rice**: Add the rinsed rice to the saucepan and cook, stirring frequently, until the rice is lightly toasted and aromatic, about 2-3 minutes.
4. **Deglaze (Optional)**: If using white wine, pour it into the saucepan and stir until it's mostly absorbed by the rice.
5. **Cook Rice**: Add the chicken or vegetable broth, dried thyme, and dried rosemary. Bring to a boil, then reduce the heat to low. Cover the saucepan with a tight-fitting lid and simmer for 15-20 minutes, or until the rice is tender and the liquid is absorbed.
6. **Fluff and Add Herbs**: Remove the saucepan from heat and let it sit, covered, for 5 minutes. Fluff the rice with a fork and stir in the chopped fresh parsley and chives (if using). Season with salt and black pepper to taste.
7. **Garnish and Serve**: If desired, garnish with slivered almonds or pine nuts for added texture and flavor. Serve warm.

This Herb-Infused Rice Pilaf is a versatile and flavorful side dish that pairs well with a variety of main courses. The combination of aromatic herbs and a touch of wine creates a savory and fragrant rice dish that's perfect for both everyday meals and special occasions.

Creamy Spinach and Mushroom Gratin

Ingredients:

- 2 tablespoons unsalted butter
- 1 small onion, finely diced
- 3 cloves garlic, minced
- 8 ounces (about 2 cups) cremini or button mushrooms, sliced
- 4 cups fresh spinach (or about 1 pound), washed and chopped
- 1 cup heavy cream
- 1 cup whole milk
- 1 cup grated Parmesan cheese
- 1/2 cup shredded Gruyère cheese (or cheddar)
- 1/4 teaspoon ground nutmeg
- 1/4 teaspoon dried thyme
- Salt and freshly ground black pepper, to taste
- 1 tablespoon all-purpose flour (optional, for thickening)
- 1/2 cup breadcrumbs (for topping)
- 2 tablespoons melted butter (for topping)
- Fresh parsley, chopped (for garnish, optional)

Instructions:

1. **Preheat Oven**: Preheat your oven to 375°F (190°C). Grease a 1.5-quart baking dish or similar-sized casserole dish.
2. **Sauté Vegetables**: In a large skillet, melt the butter over medium heat. Add the diced onion and cook until softened and translucent, about 5 minutes. Add the minced garlic and cook for another minute until fragrant.
3. **Cook Mushrooms**: Add the sliced mushrooms to the skillet and cook until they release their moisture and become golden brown, about 5-7 minutes.
4. **Add Spinach**: Stir in the chopped spinach and cook until wilted, about 2-3 minutes. Remove the skillet from heat.
5. **Prepare Cream Mixture**: In a separate saucepan, combine the heavy cream and milk. Heat gently over medium heat until warm but not boiling. If desired, whisk in the flour to thicken the mixture slightly.
6. **Combine Ingredients**: Add the grated Parmesan cheese, shredded Gruyère cheese, ground nutmeg, dried thyme, salt, and black pepper to the warm cream mixture. Stir until the cheese is melted and the mixture is smooth.
7. **Mix and Transfer**: Pour the cheese sauce over the sautéed vegetables and mix well to combine. Transfer the mixture to the prepared baking dish.
8. **Add Topping**: In a small bowl, mix the breadcrumbs with the melted butter. Sprinkle the breadcrumb mixture evenly over the top of the gratin.
9. **Bake**: Bake in the preheated oven for 25-30 minutes, or until the top is golden brown and the gratin is bubbly and hot throughout.

10. **Garnish and Serve**: Remove from the oven and let cool slightly. Garnish with chopped fresh parsley if desired.

This Creamy Spinach and Mushroom Gratin is a rich and comforting side dish, combining the earthy flavors of mushrooms with the creamy goodness of a cheese sauce and the vibrant taste of spinach. It's perfect for holiday dinners, special occasions, or as a hearty accompaniment to your favorite main courses.

Garlic Butter Shrimp

Ingredients:

- 1 pound large shrimp, peeled and deveined
- 3 tablespoons unsalted butter
- 4 cloves garlic, minced
- 1/4 teaspoon red pepper flakes (optional, for heat)
- 1/4 cup dry white wine or chicken broth
- Juice of 1 lemon
- 2 tablespoons fresh parsley, chopped
- Salt and freshly ground black pepper, to taste
- Lemon wedges (for serving, optional)

Instructions:

1. **Prepare Shrimp**: Pat the shrimp dry with paper towels. Season with salt and black pepper.
2. **Melt Butter**: In a large skillet, melt the butter over medium heat.
3. **Cook Garlic**: Add the minced garlic and red pepper flakes (if using) to the skillet. Sauté for about 1 minute, or until the garlic is fragrant but not browned.
4. **Cook Shrimp**: Add the shrimp to the skillet in a single layer. Cook for 2-3 minutes on each side, or until the shrimp are pink, opaque, and cooked through.
5. **Add Wine and Lemon Juice**: Pour in the white wine or chicken broth and lemon juice. Cook for an additional 1-2 minutes, allowing the liquid to reduce slightly and create a flavorful sauce.
6. **Finish and Serve**: Stir in the chopped fresh parsley. Taste and adjust seasoning with additional salt and pepper if needed. Serve immediately with lemon wedges on the side if desired.

This Garlic Butter Shrimp is a quick and flavorful dish that's perfect for weeknight dinners or special occasions. The combination of rich butter and aromatic garlic creates a delicious sauce that pairs beautifully with the tender shrimp.

Cranberry Pecan Salad

Ingredients:

- 6 cups mixed salad greens (such as baby spinach, arugula, and romaine)
- 1/2 cup dried cranberries
- 1/2 cup pecans, toasted
- 1/4 cup crumbled feta cheese or goat cheese
- 1 small red onion, thinly sliced
- 1 apple, cored and thinly sliced (or diced)
- 1/4 cup red onion, thinly sliced
- 1/4 cup balsamic vinaigrette or honey mustard dressing

For the Dressing (optional):

- 1/4 cup balsamic vinegar
- 1/4 cup extra-virgin olive oil
- 1 tablespoon honey or maple syrup
- 1 teaspoon Dijon mustard
- Salt and freshly ground black pepper, to taste

Instructions:

1. **Toast Pecans**: If the pecans are not already toasted, place them in a dry skillet over medium heat. Toast for 3-4 minutes, stirring frequently, until fragrant and lightly browned. Remove from heat and let cool.
2. **Prepare Salad Ingredients**: In a large salad bowl, combine the mixed salad greens, dried cranberries, toasted pecans, crumbled feta or goat cheese, sliced apple, and red onion.
3. **Make Dressing (if using homemade)**: In a small bowl or jar, whisk together balsamic vinegar, olive oil, honey or maple syrup, Dijon mustard, salt, and black pepper until well combined.
4. **Toss Salad**: Drizzle the salad with balsamic vinaigrette or your homemade dressing just before serving. Toss gently to coat all ingredients evenly.
5. **Serve**: Serve immediately, or chill the salad and dressing separately until ready to serve. Toss again before serving if the salad has been chilled.

This Cranberry Pecan Salad is a delightful blend of sweet, tangy, and savory flavors. The combination of crisp apples, crunchy pecans, and tangy cranberries makes it a refreshing and festive choice for any meal.

Roasted Red Pepper Soup

Ingredients:

- 6 large red bell peppers
- 2 tablespoons olive oil, plus extra for drizzling
- 1 medium onion, diced
- 3 cloves garlic, minced
- 1 medium carrot, peeled and diced
- 1 celery stalk, diced
- 4 cups vegetable broth or chicken broth
- 1 can (14.5 ounces) diced tomatoes
- 1/2 cup heavy cream or coconut milk
- 1 teaspoon dried basil
- 1/2 teaspoon dried thyme
- Salt and freshly ground black pepper, to taste
- 1/4 teaspoon red pepper flakes (optional, for heat)
- Fresh basil or parsley, chopped (for garnish, optional)
- Crusty bread or croutons (for serving, optional)

Instructions:

1. **Roast Peppers**: Preheat your oven to 450°F (230°C). Place the red bell peppers on a baking sheet and drizzle with olive oil. Roast in the preheated oven for 25-30 minutes, turning occasionally, until the peppers are charred and blistered. Remove from the oven and let cool. Once cooled, peel off the skins, remove the stems and seeds, and chop the peppers.
2. **Sauté Vegetables**: In a large pot, heat 2 tablespoons of olive oil over medium heat. Add the diced onion, garlic, carrot, and celery. Cook, stirring occasionally, until the vegetables are softened, about 5-7 minutes.
3. **Add Peppers and Tomatoes**: Add the roasted red peppers and canned tomatoes (with their juices) to the pot. Stir to combine.
4. **Add Broth and Herbs**: Pour in the vegetable or chicken broth, and add the dried basil, dried thyme, salt, black pepper, and red pepper flakes (if using). Bring the mixture to a boil, then reduce the heat and let it simmer for 15-20 minutes.
5. **Blend Soup**: Use an immersion blender to blend the soup until smooth. Alternatively, carefully transfer the soup in batches to a blender and blend until smooth, then return to the pot.
6. **Add Cream**: Stir in the heavy cream or coconut milk and heat through. Adjust seasoning with additional salt and pepper if needed.
7. **Serve**: Ladle the soup into bowls and garnish with chopped fresh basil or parsley, if desired. Serve with crusty bread or croutons.

This Roasted Red Pepper Soup is a creamy and flavorful dish with a rich, smoky sweetness from the roasted peppers. It's perfect as a comforting appetizer or a light meal, and pairs wonderfully with a slice of crusty bread or a simple salad.

Apple and Sausage Stuffing

Ingredients:

- 1 loaf of day-old bread (about 12 cups, cubed; preferably a mix of white and whole wheat)
- 2 tablespoons unsalted butter
- 1 pound breakfast sausage (or Italian sausage), casing removed
- 1 medium onion, finely diced
- 2 cloves garlic, minced
- 2 medium apples, peeled, cored, and diced
- 1/2 cup celery, diced
- 1/2 cup dried cranberries or raisins (optional)
- 1/2 cup chopped fresh sage (or 2 tablespoons dried sage)
- 1/2 cup chopped fresh thyme (or 2 tablespoons dried thyme)
- 2-3 cups chicken or vegetable broth (adjust as needed)
- 2 large eggs, beaten
- Salt and freshly ground black pepper, to taste

Instructions:

1. **Preheat Oven**: Preheat your oven to 350°F (175°C). Grease a 9x13-inch baking dish or similar-sized casserole dish.
2. **Prepare Bread**: If the bread is not already stale, spread the cubed bread on a baking sheet and toast in the oven for about 10-15 minutes, until slightly dried out. Transfer to a large mixing bowl.
3. **Cook Sausage**: In a large skillet, melt the butter over medium heat. Add the sausage and cook, breaking it up with a spoon, until browned and cooked through. Remove the sausage from the skillet and drain on paper towels.
4. **Sauté Vegetables and Apples**: In the same skillet, add a little more butter if needed. Add the diced onion, garlic, celery, and apples. Cook until the vegetables are softened and the apples are slightly caramelized, about 5-7 minutes.
5. **Combine Ingredients**: Add the cooked sausage back to the skillet. Stir in the dried cranberries or raisins if using, and the fresh sage and thyme. Cook for another minute until everything is well combined.
6. **Mix Stuffing**: Pour the sausage mixture over the cubed bread in the large mixing bowl. Gently toss to combine.
7. **Add Broth and Eggs**: Gradually add chicken or vegetable broth, a little at a time, until the bread is evenly moistened but not soggy. Stir in the beaten eggs. Season with salt and black pepper to taste.
8. **Transfer and Bake**: Transfer the stuffing mixture to the prepared baking dish. Cover with aluminum foil and bake in the preheated oven for 30 minutes. Remove the foil and bake for an additional 10-15 minutes, or until the top is golden brown and the stuffing is heated through.
9. **Serve**: Let the stuffing rest for a few minutes before serving.

Apple and Sausage Stuffing is a flavorful and comforting side dish that combines the savory taste of sausage with the sweetness of apples. It's a perfect addition to any holiday meal or special occasion.

Cheddar and Chive Biscuits

Ingredients:

- 2 cups all-purpose flour
- 1 tablespoon baking powder
- 1/2 teaspoon baking soda
- 1/2 teaspoon salt
- 1/2 teaspoon freshly ground black pepper
- 1/2 cup unsalted butter, cold and cut into small cubes
- 1 cup shredded sharp cheddar cheese
- 1/4 cup fresh chives, chopped
- 3/4 cup buttermilk (or regular milk with 1 tablespoon lemon juice or vinegar)
- 1 egg, beaten (for brushing, optional)

Instructions:

1. **Preheat Oven**: Preheat your oven to 425°F (220°C). Line a baking sheet with parchment paper or lightly grease it.
2. **Prepare Dry Ingredients**: In a large bowl, whisk together the flour, baking powder, baking soda, salt, and black pepper.
3. **Cut in Butter**: Add the cold, cubed butter to the flour mixture. Using a pastry cutter, two forks, or your fingers, cut the butter into the flour until the mixture resembles coarse crumbs with some pea-sized pieces of butter remaining.
4. **Add Cheese and Chives**: Stir in the shredded cheddar cheese and chopped chives until evenly distributed.
5. **Add Buttermilk**: Pour in the buttermilk and gently stir until just combined. The dough will be somewhat sticky. Avoid over-mixing to ensure tender biscuits.
6. **Shape Biscuits**: Turn the dough out onto a lightly floured surface and gently knead a few times to bring it together. Pat the dough to about 1-inch thickness. Use a biscuit cutter or a round cookie cutter to cut out biscuits, pressing straight down without twisting.
7. **Transfer and Brush**: Place the cut biscuits onto the prepared baking sheet, spacing them about 1 inch apart. If desired, brush the tops with the beaten egg for a golden finish.
8. **Bake**: Bake in the preheated oven for 12-15 minutes, or until the biscuits are golden brown on top and cooked through.
9. **Serve**: Remove from the oven and let cool slightly before serving. Enjoy warm or at room temperature.

Cheddar and Chive Biscuits are a delicious and savory addition to any meal. Their flaky, buttery texture combined with the sharpness of cheddar and the fresh flavor of chives makes them a perfect side for breakfast, brunch, or dinner.

Prosciutto-Wrapped Chicken

Ingredients:

- 4 boneless, skinless chicken breasts
- 8 slices of prosciutto
- 4 ounces cream cheese, softened
- 1/2 cup grated Parmesan cheese
- 1/2 cup fresh spinach, chopped
- 1 clove garlic, minced
- 1 tablespoon fresh thyme leaves (or 1 teaspoon dried thyme)
- 1 tablespoon olive oil
- Salt and freshly ground black pepper, to taste
- Toothpicks or kitchen twine

Instructions:

1. **Preheat Oven**: Preheat your oven to 375°F (190°C). Lightly grease a baking dish or line it with parchment paper.
2. **Prepare Filling**: In a small bowl, mix together the softened cream cheese, grated Parmesan cheese, chopped spinach, minced garlic, and fresh thyme. Season with a pinch of salt and black pepper.
3. **Prepare Chicken**: Place the chicken breasts between two sheets of plastic wrap or parchment paper. Gently pound them with a meat mallet or rolling pin to an even thickness, about 1/2 inch.
4. **Fill Chicken**: Spread a portion of the cream cheese mixture evenly over each chicken breast.
5. **Wrap with Prosciutto**: Roll up each chicken breast tightly and then wrap each one with 2 slices of prosciutto, securing with toothpicks or kitchen twine as needed.
6. **Sear Chicken**: Heat olive oil in a large skillet over medium-high heat. Add the prosciutto-wrapped chicken and sear for 2-3 minutes per side, until the prosciutto is crisp and the chicken is golden brown.
7. **Bake Chicken**: Transfer the seared chicken breasts to the prepared baking dish. Bake in the preheated oven for 20-25 minutes, or until the chicken is cooked through and reaches an internal temperature of 165°F (74°C).
8. **Rest and Serve**: Remove the chicken from the oven and let it rest for 5 minutes before removing the toothpicks or twine. Serve warm.

This Prosciutto-Wrapped Chicken is a savory and elegant dish, perfect for a special dinner or a weeknight meal. The prosciutto adds a delightful crispiness and rich flavor to the tender chicken, while the cream cheese filling provides a creamy and flavorful surprise inside.

Roasted Beet and Goat Cheese Salad

Ingredients:

- 4 medium beets, trimmed and scrubbed
- 2 tablespoons olive oil
- Salt and freshly ground black pepper, to taste
- 4 cups mixed salad greens (such as baby spinach, arugula, and/or mesclun)
- 4 ounces goat cheese, crumbled
- 1/2 cup walnuts, toasted and chopped
- Balsamic vinegar or balsamic glaze, for drizzling

Instructions:

1. **Roast Beets**: Preheat your oven to 400°F (200°C). Place the trimmed and scrubbed beets on a large piece of aluminum foil. Drizzle with olive oil and season with salt and pepper. Wrap the beets tightly in the foil and place on a baking sheet. Roast in the preheated oven for 45-60 minutes, or until the beets are tender when pierced with a fork. Let them cool slightly, then peel and cut into wedges or slices.
2. **Prepare Salad**: Arrange the mixed salad greens on a serving platter or individual plates. Top with the roasted beet wedges or slices.
3. **Add Toppings**: Sprinkle the crumbled goat cheese and chopped walnuts over the salad greens and roasted beets.
4. **Drizzle with Balsamic**: Just before serving, drizzle with balsamic vinegar or balsamic glaze for added flavor and presentation.
5. **Serve**: Serve immediately as a delicious and colorful salad that combines the earthy sweetness of roasted beets with creamy goat cheese, crunchy walnuts, and tangy balsamic drizzle.

This Roasted Beet and Goat Cheese Salad is a vibrant and flavorful dish that makes a perfect appetizer or light meal. It's packed with nutrients and textures, making it both satisfying and refreshing.

Brown Sugar Glazed Carrots

Ingredients:

- 1 pound carrots, peeled and sliced into coins or sticks
- 2 tablespoons unsalted butter
- 1/4 cup brown sugar
- 1/4 cup water or vegetable broth
- Salt and freshly ground black pepper, to taste
- Fresh parsley, chopped (for garnish, optional)

Instructions:

1. **Cook Carrots**: In a large skillet or saucepan, melt the butter over medium heat. Add the sliced carrots and cook for about 5 minutes, stirring occasionally, until they start to soften.
2. **Add Brown Sugar and Liquid**: Sprinkle the brown sugar over the carrots and stir to coat evenly. Pour in the water or vegetable broth, and season with salt and black pepper to taste.
3. **Simmer**: Bring the mixture to a simmer. Reduce the heat to medium-low and continue to cook, uncovered, for 10-15 minutes or until the carrots are tender and the liquid has reduced to a glaze, stirring occasionally.
4. **Finish and Serve**: Remove from heat and let the carrots sit for a few minutes to allow the glaze to thicken slightly. Stir gently to coat the carrots in the glaze.
5. **Garnish and Serve**: Transfer the glazed carrots to a serving dish. Garnish with chopped fresh parsley if desired. Serve warm as a delicious side dish.

These Brown Sugar Glazed Carrots are a sweet and savory treat that complements a variety of main dishes. The brown sugar adds caramelized sweetness to the tender carrots, making them a perfect addition to your holiday table or everyday meals.

Herbed Cream Cheese Mashed Potatoes

Ingredients:

- 2 pounds potatoes (such as Yukon Gold or Russet), peeled and cut into chunks
- Salt, for cooking potatoes
- 1/2 cup cream cheese, softened
- 1/2 cup sour cream
- 1/4 cup unsalted butter
- 1/4 cup milk or cream
- 2 cloves garlic, minced
- 2 tablespoons fresh herbs (such as parsley, chives, or thyme), chopped
- Salt and freshly ground black pepper, to taste
- Optional: additional butter and herbs for garnish

Instructions:

1. **Cook Potatoes**: Place the peeled and cut potatoes in a large pot and cover with cold water. Add a generous pinch of salt. Bring to a boil over medium-high heat, then reduce the heat to medium-low and simmer for 15-20 minutes, or until the potatoes are fork-tender.
2. **Prepare Cream Cheese Mixture**: While the potatoes are cooking, in a small bowl, mix together the softened cream cheese, sour cream, and butter until smooth and well combined.
3. **Drain and Mash Potatoes**: Drain the cooked potatoes thoroughly and return them to the pot. Mash the potatoes using a potato masher or a hand mixer until smooth and creamy.
4. **Add Cream Cheese Mixture**: Add the cream cheese mixture to the mashed potatoes. Stir or beat until well incorporated.
5. **Add Garlic and Herbs**: Stir in the minced garlic and chopped fresh herbs. Season with salt and black pepper to taste.
6. **Adjust Consistency**: Gradually add milk or cream, a little at a time, until the mashed potatoes reach your desired creamy consistency. Be careful not to overmix.
7. **Serve**: Transfer the herbed cream cheese mashed potatoes to a serving bowl. Optionally, garnish with additional butter and chopped herbs before serving.

These Herbed Cream Cheese Mashed Potatoes are rich, creamy, and infused with the flavors of fresh herbs and tangy cream cheese. They make a wonderful side dish for any occasion, adding a delicious twist to classic mashed potatoes that your guests will love.

Sweet and Sour Glazed Ham

Ingredients:

- 1 fully cooked bone-in ham (about 8-10 pounds)
- 1 cup brown sugar
- 1/2 cup honey
- 1/2 cup Dijon mustard
- 1/4 cup apple cider vinegar
- 1/4 cup pineapple juice
- 1 teaspoon ground cloves
- 1/2 teaspoon ground cinnamon
- 1/4 teaspoon ground nutmeg
- 1/4 teaspoon ground ginger
- Pineapple rings and maraschino cherries for garnish (optional)

Instructions:

1. **Preheat Oven**: Preheat your oven to 325°F (160°C).
2. **Prepare Ham**: Place the ham on a large roasting pan lined with foil. Score the surface of the ham in a diamond pattern with a sharp knife, about 1/4-inch deep.
3. **Make Glaze**: In a saucepan, combine brown sugar, honey, Dijon mustard, apple cider vinegar, pineapple juice, ground cloves, cinnamon, nutmeg, and ginger. Bring to a simmer over medium heat, stirring occasionally. Reduce heat and let the glaze simmer for about 5-7 minutes until slightly thickened.
4. **Glaze Ham**: Brush half of the glaze over the ham, making sure to get into the scored cuts. Reserve the remaining glaze for basting.
5. **Bake Ham**: Bake the ham in the preheated oven, uncovered, for about 1.5 to 2 hours, or until the internal temperature reaches 140°F (60°C), basting with the remaining glaze every 30 minutes.
6. **Rest and Garnish**: Remove the ham from the oven and let it rest for about 15 minutes before slicing. Garnish with pineapple rings and maraschino cherries if desired.
7. **Serve**: Slice and serve the sweet and sour glazed ham warm. Enjoy the deliciously flavored ham with its caramelized glaze.

This Sweet and Sour Glazed Ham is a classic and flavorful dish that is perfect for holiday dinners or special occasions. The combination of sweet honey, tangy mustard, and aromatic spices creates a delicious glaze that enhances the natural flavors of the ham, making it a favorite among guests and family alike.

Butternut Squash and Sage Ravioli

Ingredients:

For the pasta dough (you can also use store-bought wonton wrappers for convenience):

- 2 cups all-purpose flour
- 3 large eggs
- 1/2 teaspoon salt

For the filling:

- 2 cups butternut squash, peeled and cubed
- 1 tablespoon olive oil
- Salt and freshly ground black pepper, to taste
- 1/4 cup ricotta cheese
- 1/4 cup grated Parmesan cheese
- 1/4 teaspoon ground nutmeg
- 1 tablespoon fresh sage, chopped

For the sauce:

- 4 tablespoons unsalted butter
- 8-10 fresh sage leaves
- 1/4 cup grated Parmesan cheese (optional)

Instructions:

1. **Prepare the Pasta Dough:**
   - On a clean surface, mound the flour and make a well in the center. Crack the eggs into the well and add salt.
   - Using a fork, gradually incorporate the flour into the eggs until a dough forms. Knead the dough for about 5-10 minutes until smooth and elastic. Wrap in plastic wrap and let it rest for 30 minutes.
2. **Roast the Butternut Squash:**
   - Preheat your oven to 400°F (200°C). Toss the cubed butternut squash with olive oil, salt, and pepper on a baking sheet.
   - Roast in the preheated oven for 20-25 minutes, or until tender and lightly caramelized. Let cool slightly.
3. **Make the Filling:**
   - In a food processor, combine the roasted butternut squash, ricotta cheese, Parmesan cheese, nutmeg, and chopped sage. Pulse until smooth. Season with salt and pepper to taste.
4. **Roll Out the Pasta Dough:**

- Divide the rested pasta dough into smaller portions. Roll out each portion using a pasta machine or a rolling pin until very thin (about 1/16 inch thick). If using store-bought wonton wrappers, skip this step.

5. **Assemble the Ravioli:**
   - Place teaspoons of the butternut squash filling onto one sheet of pasta dough or wonton wrapper, leaving about 1 inch between each mound of filling.
   - Brush the edges of the pasta or wonton wrapper with water and place another sheet of pasta or wrapper on top. Press down around each mound of filling to seal and remove any air bubbles. Use a knife or a ravioli cutter to cut out individual ravioli squares or circles.
6. **Cook the Ravioli:**
   - Bring a large pot of salted water to a boil. Add the ravioli in batches and cook for about 3-4 minutes, or until they float to the surface and are tender. Remove with a slotted spoon and set aside.
7. **Make the Sage Butter Sauce:**
   - In a large skillet, melt the butter over medium heat until it begins to foam. Add the sage leaves and cook until crisp, about 1-2 minutes.
   - Add the cooked ravioli to the skillet and gently toss to coat in the sage butter sauce.
8. **Serve:**
   - Divide the ravioli among plates or bowls. Drizzle with any remaining sage butter sauce from the skillet. Sprinkle with grated Parmesan cheese if desired. Serve immediately.

This Butternut Squash and Sage Ravioli dish is a delightful blend of sweet butternut squash filling and savory sage butter sauce, making it a perfect comfort food for any occasion.

Maple-Dijon Glazed Pork Tenderloin

Ingredients:

- 2 pork tenderloins (about 1 pound each)
- Salt and freshly ground black pepper, to taste
- 1/4 cup Dijon mustard
- 1/4 cup maple syrup
- 2 tablespoons olive oil
- 2 cloves garlic, minced
- 1 tablespoon fresh rosemary, chopped (or 1 teaspoon dried rosemary)
- 1 tablespoon fresh thyme leaves (or 1 teaspoon dried thyme)
- Optional: 1 tablespoon soy sauce or Worcestershire sauce for added depth (optional)

Instructions:

1. **Preheat Oven and Prepare Pork:**
    - Preheat your oven to 400°F (200°C). Pat the pork tenderloins dry with paper towels and season them generously with salt and pepper.
2. **Make Glaze:**
    - In a small bowl, whisk together the Dijon mustard, maple syrup, olive oil, minced garlic, chopped rosemary, and thyme. Add soy sauce or Worcestershire sauce if using.
3. **Coat Pork:**
    - Brush the pork tenderloins all over with the maple-Dijon glaze, reserving some for basting during cooking.
4. **Sear Pork (Optional):**
    - Heat a large oven-safe skillet or frying pan over medium-high heat. Add a tablespoon of olive oil and sear the pork tenderloins until browned on all sides, about 2-3 minutes per side. This step is optional but adds extra flavor and texture to the pork.
5. **Roast Pork:**
    - Transfer the skillet or pork tenderloins to the preheated oven. Roast for 15-20 minutes, or until the internal temperature reaches 145°F (63°C) for medium-rare to medium doneness, or 160°F (71°C) for medium-well.
6. **Baste and Rest:**
    - During the last 5-10 minutes of cooking, baste the pork tenderloins with the remaining maple-Dijon glaze. Remove from the oven and let the pork rest for 5-10 minutes before slicing.
7. **Slice and Serve:**
    - Slice the pork tenderloins into medallions and serve with any remaining glaze drizzled over the top. Garnish with fresh herbs if desired.

This Maple-Dijon Glazed Pork Tenderloin recipe results in tender, juicy pork with a sweet and savory flavor profile. It's perfect for a special dinner or holiday meal, paired with your favorite sides like roasted vegetables or mashed potatoes.

Parmesan-Crusted Cauliflower

Ingredients:

- 1 large head of cauliflower, cut into florets
- 1 cup breadcrumbs (preferably panko)
- 1 cup grated Parmesan cheese
- 1 teaspoon garlic powder
- 1 teaspoon dried oregano
- 1/2 teaspoon smoked paprika
- Salt and freshly ground black pepper, to taste
- 2 large eggs, beaten
- Cooking spray or olive oil

Instructions:

1. **Preheat Oven**: Preheat your oven to 400°F (200°C). Line a baking sheet with parchment paper or lightly grease it with cooking spray or olive oil.
2. **Prepare Cauliflower**: Cut the cauliflower into florets. Make sure they are bite-sized pieces for easy handling.
3. **Prepare Breading Station**: In a shallow bowl or dish, combine breadcrumbs, grated Parmesan cheese, garlic powder, dried oregano, smoked paprika, salt, and black pepper. Mix well.
4. **Coat Cauliflower**: Dip each cauliflower floret into the beaten eggs, letting any excess drip off. Then coat the floret thoroughly in the breadcrumb-Parmesan mixture, pressing gently to adhere.
5. **Arrange on Baking Sheet**: Place the coated cauliflower florets in a single layer on the prepared baking sheet. Leave a little space between each piece to ensure they crisp up evenly.
6. **Bake**: Bake in the preheated oven for 20-25 minutes, flipping halfway through, until the cauliflower is tender and the coating is golden brown and crispy.
7. **Serve**: Remove from the oven and let cool slightly before serving. Garnish with additional grated Parmesan cheese and fresh herbs if desired. Serve warm as a delicious and crispy side dish or appetizer.

This Parmesan-Crusted Cauliflower recipe is a fantastic way to enjoy cauliflower with a crispy and flavorful coating. It's a healthier alternative to fried snacks and pairs well with various dipping sauces or as a side dish for any meal.

Cranberry Stuffed Pork Loin

Ingredients:

- 1 pork loin roast (about 3-4 pounds)
- Salt and freshly ground black pepper, to taste
- 1 tablespoon olive oil

For the stuffing:

- 1 cup fresh or frozen cranberries
- 1/2 cup dried cranberries
- 1/2 cup pecans, chopped
- 1/4 cup brown sugar
- 1 tablespoon orange zest
- 1/2 teaspoon ground cinnamon
- 1/4 teaspoon ground nutmeg
- 1/4 teaspoon ground cloves
- 1/4 teaspoon salt
- 1/4 cup orange juice

For the glaze (optional):

- 1/4 cup cranberry sauce
- 2 tablespoons maple syrup or honey
- 1 tablespoon Dijon mustard

Instructions:

1. **Prepare the Pork Loin:**
    - Preheat your oven to 375°F (190°C). Butterfly the pork loin by making a lengthwise cut down the center, without cutting all the way through, so you can open it like a book. Season both sides with salt and pepper.
2. **Make the Stuffing:**
    - In a bowl, combine the fresh cranberries, dried cranberries, chopped pecans, brown sugar, orange zest, ground cinnamon, nutmeg, cloves, and salt. Mix well. Spread this mixture evenly over the butterflied pork loin.
3. **Roll and Tie the Loin:**
    - Starting at one end, roll up the pork loin tightly with the stuffing inside. Use kitchen twine to tie the roast at intervals to secure the stuffing inside.
4. **Sear the Pork Loin (Optional):**
    - Heat olive oil in a large oven-safe skillet over medium-high heat. Sear the stuffed pork loin on all sides until browned, about 2-3 minutes per side. This step adds flavor and helps seal in juices.
5. **Bake the Pork Loin:**

- Place the seared or unseared pork loin in a roasting pan or oven-safe skillet. Roast in the preheated oven for 60-75 minutes, or until the internal temperature reaches 145°F (63°C) for medium rare or 160°F (71°C) for medium.

6. **Make the Glaze (Optional):**
   - In a small saucepan, combine cranberry sauce, maple syrup or honey, and Dijon mustard. Cook over medium heat, stirring occasionally, until warmed through and well combined.

7. **Glaze and Serve:**
   - During the last 10-15 minutes of cooking, brush the pork loin with the cranberry glaze. Continue roasting until the glaze is caramelized and the pork is cooked through.

8. **Rest and Slice:**
   - Remove the pork loin from the oven and let it rest for 10-15 minutes before slicing. Remove the kitchen twine and slice the stuffed pork loin into thick slices. Serve warm, drizzled with any remaining cranberry glaze.

This Cranberry Stuffed Pork Loin recipe is a festive and flavorful dish that combines the savory pork with the sweet-tartness of cranberries and pecans. It's perfect for holiday dinners or special occasions, impressing guests with its beautiful presentation and delicious taste.

Lemon-Garlic Roasted Chicken

Ingredients:

- 1 whole chicken (about 4-5 pounds), giblets removed
- 2 lemons, divided
- 4 cloves garlic, minced
- 2 tablespoons olive oil
- 1 tablespoon fresh thyme leaves (or 1 teaspoon dried thyme)
- 1 tablespoon fresh rosemary leaves (or 1 teaspoon dried rosemary)
- Salt and freshly ground black pepper, to taste
- Optional: 1 teaspoon paprika or smoked paprika for extra flavor

Instructions:

1. **Preheat Oven**: Preheat your oven to 425°F (220°C).
2. **Prepare Chicken**: Pat the chicken dry with paper towels. Season the cavity with salt and pepper. Cut one lemon into wedges and stuff them inside the cavity of the chicken.
3. **Make the Marinade**: In a small bowl, combine the minced garlic, olive oil, juice of the remaining lemon, thyme leaves, rosemary leaves, salt, pepper, and paprika if using. Mix well.
4. **Coat Chicken**: Rub the marinade mixture all over the chicken, ensuring it's evenly coated, including under the skin if possible. Tie the legs together with kitchen twine for even cooking.
5. **Roast Chicken**: Place the chicken breast-side up on a roasting pan or baking dish. Roast in the preheated oven for about 1 hour to 1 hour 15 minutes, or until the juices run clear and the internal temperature of the thickest part of the thigh reaches 165°F (74°C).
6. **Baste Chicken**: Every 20-30 minutes during cooking, baste the chicken with the pan juices or additional marinade to keep it moist and flavorful.
7. **Rest and Serve**: Remove the chicken from the oven and let it rest for 10-15 minutes before carving. This allows the juices to redistribute, ensuring a juicy chicken.
8. **Carve and Garnish**: Carve the roasted chicken into pieces. Serve with roasted vegetables, rice, or salad. Garnish with fresh herbs and lemon wedges if desired.

This Lemon-Garlic Roasted Chicken recipe results in a tender and flavorful dish with crispy skin and juicy meat infused with the zesty flavors of lemon and garlic. It's perfect for a family dinner or special occasion, impressing everyone with its delicious aroma and taste.

Spiced Apple Chutney

Ingredients:

- 4 cups apples, peeled, cored, and chopped (about 4-5 medium apples)
- 1 cup onion, finely chopped
- 1 cup apple cider vinegar
- 1 cup brown sugar
- 1/2 cup raisins or dried cranberries
- 1/2 cup chopped dates
- 1/4 cup crystallized ginger, finely chopped
- 1 tablespoon mustard seeds
- 1 teaspoon ground cinnamon
- 1/2 teaspoon ground cloves
- 1/2 teaspoon ground nutmeg
- 1/2 teaspoon salt
- 1/4 teaspoon cayenne pepper (optional, for heat)
- 1/4 cup water (optional, for consistency)

Instructions:

1. **Prepare Ingredients**: Peel, core, and chop the apples. Finely chop the onion and crystallized ginger.
2. **Cook Chutney**: In a large saucepan or pot, combine the chopped apples, chopped onion, apple cider vinegar, brown sugar, raisins or dried cranberries, chopped dates, crystallized ginger, mustard seeds, ground cinnamon, ground cloves, ground nutmeg, salt, and cayenne pepper if using.
3. **Simmer**: Bring the mixture to a boil over medium-high heat, stirring occasionally. Reduce the heat to low and simmer, uncovered, stirring occasionally, for about 45 minutes to 1 hour. The chutney should thicken and the flavors meld together.
4. **Adjust Consistency**: If the chutney becomes too thick during cooking, you can add water, 1/4 cup at a time, to achieve your desired consistency.
5. **Cool and Store**: Remove the pot from heat and let the spiced apple chutney cool to room temperature. Transfer to sterilized jars or airtight containers and store in the refrigerator.
6. **Serve**: Serve the spiced apple chutney as a condiment with roasted meats (such as pork or chicken), cheeses, sandwiches, or as a topping for crackers. Enjoy the sweet and tangy flavors!

This Spiced Apple Chutney is a delightful preserve that combines the sweetness of apples with the warmth of spices and a hint of tanginess from vinegar. It's versatile and adds a flavorful touch to various dishes, making it a wonderful addition to your pantry or a thoughtful homemade gift.

Baked Macaroni and Cheese

Ingredients:

- 8 ounces elbow macaroni (or any pasta shape you prefer)
- 4 tablespoons unsalted butter
- 1/4 cup all-purpose flour
- 2 cups milk (preferably whole milk)
- 2 cups shredded sharp cheddar cheese
- 1 cup shredded mozzarella cheese (or another cheese of your choice)
- 1/2 teaspoon salt, or to taste
- 1/4 teaspoon black pepper, or to taste
- 1/4 teaspoon ground mustard (optional, for extra flavor)
- 1/4 teaspoon paprika (optional, for color and flavor)
- 1/2 cup breadcrumbs (optional, for topping)
- Fresh chopped parsley or chives, for garnish (optional)

Instructions:

1. **Preheat Oven and Cook Pasta**: Preheat your oven to 350°F (175°C). Cook the elbow macaroni according to package instructions until al dente. Drain and set aside.
2. **Make Cheese Sauce**: In a large saucepan, melt the butter over medium heat. Stir in the flour and cook for 1-2 minutes until bubbly and lightly golden, stirring constantly.
3. **Add Milk**: Gradually whisk in the milk, a little at a time, until smooth and combined. Cook, stirring constantly, until the mixture thickens and comes to a simmer, about 5-7 minutes.
4. **Add Cheese**: Remove the saucepan from heat. Stir in the shredded cheddar cheese and shredded mozzarella cheese until melted and smooth. Season with salt, black pepper, ground mustard (if using), and paprika (if using).
5. **Combine Pasta and Cheese Sauce**: Add the cooked elbow macaroni to the cheese sauce, stirring until well coated.
6. **Bake**: Transfer the macaroni and cheese mixture to a greased baking dish. Sprinkle breadcrumbs evenly over the top, if using.
7. **Bake**: Bake in the preheated oven for 25-30 minutes, or until the top is golden brown and the edges are bubbly.
8. **Serve**: Remove from the oven and let it cool for a few minutes. Garnish with fresh chopped parsley or chives if desired. Serve warm as a comforting and cheesy main dish or side.

This Baked Macaroni and Cheese recipe is creamy, cheesy, and comforting, making it a favorite for both kids and adults alike. It's perfect for a family dinner or potluck, offering a deliciously satisfying meal with its gooey cheese and crispy breadcrumb topping.

Winter Salad with Pomegranate Vinaigrette

Ingredients:

For the salad:

- 6 cups mixed salad greens (such as arugula, spinach, or mixed baby greens)
- 1 cup sliced red cabbage
- 1 cup shredded carrots
- 1/2 cup sliced red onion
- 1/2 cup pomegranate arils (seeds)
- 1/4 cup toasted pecans or walnuts
- 1/4 cup crumbled feta cheese (optional)
- Salt and freshly ground black pepper, to taste

For the pomegranate vinaigrette:

- 1/4 cup pomegranate juice (freshly squeezed or store-bought)
- 2 tablespoons red wine vinegar
- 1 tablespoon honey or maple syrup
- 1/2 teaspoon Dijon mustard
- 1/4 cup olive oil
- Salt and freshly ground black pepper, to taste

Instructions:

1. **Prepare the Salad Greens**: In a large salad bowl, combine the mixed salad greens, sliced red cabbage, shredded carrots, sliced red onion, and pomegranate arils.
2. **Make the Pomegranate Vinaigrette**: In a small bowl or jar, whisk together the pomegranate juice, red wine vinegar, honey or maple syrup, and Dijon mustard until well combined. Gradually whisk in the olive oil until emulsified. Season with salt and pepper to taste.
3. **Assemble the Salad**: Drizzle the desired amount of pomegranate vinaigrette over the salad greens and gently toss to coat evenly. Season with additional salt and pepper if needed.
4. **Add Toppings**: Sprinkle toasted pecans or walnuts and crumbled feta cheese (if using) over the top of the salad.
5. **Serve**: Serve the winter salad immediately as a refreshing and colorful side dish or add grilled chicken or shrimp to make it a complete meal.

This Winter Salad with Pomegranate Vinaigrette is vibrant, flavorful, and packed with seasonal ingredients. The combination of crunchy vegetables, juicy pomegranate arils, and tangy-sweet vinaigrette creates a perfect balance of flavors and textures, making it a delightful addition to any winter meal or holiday table.

Savory Pumpkin Risotto

Ingredients:

- 1 cup Arborio rice (risotto rice)
- 4 cups chicken or vegetable broth
- 1 cup canned pumpkin puree
- 1/2 cup dry white wine
- 1/2 cup grated Parmesan cheese
- 1 small onion, finely chopped
- 2 cloves garlic, minced
- 2 tablespoons unsalted butter
- 2 tablespoons olive oil
- 1/2 teaspoon ground nutmeg
- 1/2 teaspoon dried sage
- Salt and freshly ground black pepper, to taste
- Fresh parsley, chopped, for garnish

Instructions:

1. **Prepare the Broth**: In a saucepan, heat the chicken or vegetable broth until simmering. Keep it warm over low heat.
2. **Sauté Onion and Garlic**: In a large, deep skillet or Dutch oven, heat the olive oil and 1 tablespoon of butter over medium heat. Add the finely chopped onion and minced garlic. Sauté for 3-4 minutes until softened and translucent.
3. **Toast the Rice**: Add the Arborio rice to the skillet with the onion and garlic. Stir and cook for about 1-2 minutes until the rice becomes slightly translucent around the edges.
4. **Deglaze with Wine**: Pour in the dry white wine and cook, stirring constantly, until the wine is absorbed by the rice.
5. **Add Pumpkin Puree**: Stir in the canned pumpkin puree, ground nutmeg, and dried sage until well combined.
6. **Cook the Risotto**: Ladle in about 1 cup of warm broth into the skillet with the rice. Stir frequently over medium heat until the broth is absorbed. Repeat this process, adding 1 cup of broth at a time, and stirring until each addition is absorbed before adding the next. This process will take about 20-25 minutes until the rice is creamy and tender, but still slightly firm to the bite (al dente).
7. **Finish with Cheese and Butter**: Once the rice is cooked to your desired consistency, stir in the grated Parmesan cheese and remaining tablespoon of butter. Season with salt and pepper to taste.
8. **Serve**: Remove the skillet from heat. Garnish the savory pumpkin risotto with chopped fresh parsley. Serve immediately as a delicious and comforting main dish or side.

This Savory Pumpkin Risotto recipe is perfect for fall and winter, showcasing the creamy texture of Arborio rice combined with the earthy sweetness of pumpkin and the warmth of nutmeg and sage. It's a hearty and satisfying dish that pairs well with roasted vegetables or grilled chicken for a complete meal. Enjoy the flavors of the season in every creamy spoonful!

Spicy Sausage and Chestnut Stuffing

Ingredients:

- 1 loaf of day-old bread (about 1 pound), cut into 1/2-inch cubes
- 1/2 cup (1 stick) unsalted butter
- 1 lb spicy Italian sausage, casing removed
- 1 large onion, chopped
- 3-4 cloves garlic, minced
- 2 celery stalks, chopped
- 1 tablespoon fresh sage, chopped (or 1 teaspoon dried sage)
- 1 tablespoon fresh thyme leaves (or 1 teaspoon dried thyme)
- 1/2 teaspoon ground nutmeg
- Salt and freshly ground black pepper, to taste
- 2 cups roasted chestnuts, chopped
- 1/2 cup fresh parsley, chopped
- 1-2 cups chicken or vegetable broth
- Optional: 1 cup dried cranberries or chopped apples for added sweetness and texture

Instructions:

1. **Prepare Bread Cubes:**
    - Preheat your oven to 300°F (150°C). Spread the bread cubes in a single layer on a baking sheet. Bake for 15-20 minutes, tossing occasionally, until the bread cubes are dry and lightly toasted. Remove from the oven and let cool.
2. **Cook Sausage:**
    - In a large skillet or frying pan, melt 2 tablespoons of butter over medium heat. Add the spicy Italian sausage, breaking it into smaller pieces with a spoon. Cook until browned and cooked through, about 5-7 minutes. Remove the sausage from the pan and set aside.
3. **Sauté Vegetables:**
    - In the same skillet, melt the remaining butter over medium heat. Add the chopped onion, garlic, and celery. Cook, stirring occasionally, until the vegetables are softened and translucent, about 5-6 minutes.
4. **Add Herbs and Spices:**
    - Stir in the chopped fresh sage, thyme leaves, ground nutmeg, salt, and black pepper. Cook for another 1-2 minutes until fragrant.
5. **Combine Ingredients:**
    - In a large mixing bowl, combine the toasted bread cubes, cooked spicy sausage, sautéed vegetables and herbs, chopped roasted chestnuts, and fresh parsley. Add dried cranberries or chopped apples if desired for added sweetness and texture.
6. **Moisten with Broth:**

- Gradually pour chicken or vegetable broth over the stuffing mixture, starting with 1 cup and adding more as needed, until the stuffing is moistened but not soggy. The amount of broth may vary depending on how dry your bread cubes are.

7. **Bake:**
    - Preheat your oven to 350°F (175°C). Transfer the stuffing mixture to a greased baking dish. Cover with foil and bake for 30 minutes. Remove the foil and bake for an additional 15-20 minutes, or until the top is golden brown and crispy.

8. **Serve:**
    - Remove from the oven and let the spicy sausage and chestnut stuffing rest for 5-10 minutes before serving. Garnish with additional chopped parsley if desired. Serve warm as a delicious side dish for Thanksgiving, Christmas, or any holiday meal.

This Spicy Sausage and Chestnut Stuffing recipe combines savory Italian sausage with the rich flavors of roasted chestnuts and aromatic herbs, creating a deliciously hearty and flavorful dish that's perfect for festive gatherings and special occasions.

Roasted Garlic and Herb Mushrooms

Ingredients:

- 1 lb (450g) mushrooms, such as cremini or button mushrooms, cleaned and quartered
- 4 cloves garlic, minced
- 2 tablespoons olive oil
- 1 tablespoon balsamic vinegar
- 1 teaspoon dried thyme (or 1 tablespoon fresh thyme leaves)
- 1 teaspoon dried rosemary (or 1 tablespoon fresh rosemary leaves, chopped)
- Salt and freshly ground black pepper, to taste
- Fresh parsley, chopped, for garnish

Instructions:

1. **Preheat Oven:** Preheat your oven to 400°F (200°C).
2. **Prepare Mushrooms:** In a large bowl, combine the quartered mushrooms with minced garlic, olive oil, balsamic vinegar, dried thyme, dried rosemary, salt, and black pepper. Toss until the mushrooms are evenly coated with the seasonings.
3. **Roast Mushrooms:** Spread the seasoned mushrooms in a single layer on a baking sheet lined with parchment paper or aluminum foil.
4. **Bake:** Roast in the preheated oven for 20-25 minutes, stirring once halfway through, until the mushrooms are tender and golden brown.
5. **Garnish and Serve:** Remove from the oven and transfer the roasted garlic and herb mushrooms to a serving dish. Garnish with fresh chopped parsley. Serve warm as a delicious side dish or appetizer.

This Roasted Garlic and Herb Mushrooms recipe is simple yet bursting with flavor from the garlic, herbs, and balsamic vinegar. It makes a fantastic addition to any meal, whether served alongside grilled meats, tossed into salads, or enjoyed on their own as a savory snack.

Creamy Buttermilk Mashed Potatoes

Ingredients:

- 2 lbs (about 1 kg) potatoes (such as Yukon Gold or Russet), peeled and cut into chunks
- Salt, to taste
- 1/2 cup buttermilk
- 1/4 cup unsalted butter, cut into cubes
- 1/4 cup sour cream
- Freshly ground black pepper, to taste
- Chopped fresh chives or parsley, for garnish (optional)

Instructions:

1. **Cook Potatoes:** Place the peeled and chopped potatoes in a large pot and cover with cold water. Add a generous pinch of salt to the water. Bring to a boil over medium-high heat, then reduce the heat to medium-low and simmer until the potatoes are tender when pierced with a fork, about 15-20 minutes.
2. **Warm Buttermilk and Butter:** While the potatoes are cooking, in a small saucepan, heat the buttermilk and butter over low heat until the butter is melted and the mixture is warm. Remove from heat.
3. **Drain and Mash Potatoes:** Drain the cooked potatoes well and return them to the pot. Using a potato masher or a potato ricer, mash the potatoes until smooth and free of lumps.
4. **Add Buttermilk Mixture:** Gradually pour the warm buttermilk and butter mixture into the mashed potatoes, stirring gently to combine.
5. **Add Sour Cream and Season:** Stir in the sour cream until well combined. Season with salt and freshly ground black pepper to taste. Adjust consistency with more buttermilk if needed.
6. **Serve:** Transfer the creamy buttermilk mashed potatoes to a serving bowl. Garnish with chopped fresh chives or parsley if desired. Serve warm as a comforting side dish.

These creamy buttermilk mashed potatoes are rich, flavorful, and have a tangy twist from the buttermilk that adds a delightful depth of flavor. They pair perfectly with roasted meats, poultry, or as part of a holiday feast. Enjoy the velvety texture and delicious taste of these mashed potatoes!

Honey-Balsamic Roasted Carrots

Ingredients:

- 1 lb (450g) carrots, peeled and trimmed
- 2 tablespoons olive oil
- 2 tablespoons balsamic vinegar
- 2 tablespoons honey
- 2 cloves garlic, minced
- 1 teaspoon dried thyme (or 1 tablespoon fresh thyme leaves)
- Salt and freshly ground black pepper, to taste
- Fresh parsley, chopped, for garnish (optional)

Instructions:

1. **Preheat Oven:** Preheat your oven to 400°F (200°C).
2. **Prepare Carrots:** In a large bowl, toss the peeled and trimmed carrots with olive oil, balsamic vinegar, honey, minced garlic, dried thyme, salt, and black pepper until evenly coated.
3. **Roast Carrots:** Spread the seasoned carrots in a single layer on a baking sheet lined with parchment paper or aluminum foil.
4. **Bake:** Roast in the preheated oven for 20-25 minutes, stirring once halfway through, until the carrots are tender and caramelized.
5. **Garnish and Serve:** Remove from the oven and transfer the honey-balsamic roasted carrots to a serving dish. Garnish with chopped fresh parsley if desired. Serve warm as a delicious side dish.

These Honey-Balsamic Roasted Carrots are a delightful blend of sweet and tangy flavors, enhanced by the caramelization from roasting. They make a perfect accompaniment to roasted meats, poultry, or as part of a vegetarian meal. Enjoy the vibrant colors and delicious taste of these roasted carrots!

Mushroom and Gruyere Stuffed Beef Wellington

Ingredients:

- 1 1/2 lbs (680g) beef tenderloin, trimmed
- Salt and freshly ground black pepper, to taste
- 2 tablespoons olive oil
- 1 lb (450g) mushrooms (such as cremini or button), finely chopped
- 3 cloves garlic, minced
- 1 tablespoon fresh thyme leaves (or 1 teaspoon dried thyme)
- 1 tablespoon fresh parsley, chopped
- 1/2 cup grated Gruyere cheese
- 1 sheet puff pastry, thawed if frozen
- 1 egg, beaten (for egg wash)
- Dijon mustard, for brushing

Instructions:

1. **Preheat Oven:** Preheat your oven to 400°F (200°C).
2. **Season and Sear Beef:** Season the beef tenderloin generously with salt and pepper. In a large skillet, heat olive oil over medium-high heat. Sear the beef tenderloin on all sides until browned, about 2-3 minutes per side. Remove from heat and let it cool slightly.
3. **Prepare Mushroom Mixture:** In the same skillet, add more olive oil if needed. Sauté the chopped mushrooms until they release their moisture and become tender, about 5-7 minutes. Add minced garlic, thyme, and parsley. Cook for another 1-2 minutes until fragrant. Season with salt and pepper to taste. Remove from heat and let it cool.
4. **Assemble Beef Wellington:** Roll out the puff pastry on a lightly floured surface into a rectangle large enough to wrap the beef tenderloin. Spread a thin layer of Dijon mustard over the puff pastry. Spread the cooled mushroom mixture evenly over the mustard. Sprinkle grated Gruyere cheese on top of the mushrooms.
5. **Wrap Beef:** Place the seared beef tenderloin on top of the mushroom and cheese layer. Carefully wrap the puff pastry around the beef, sealing the seams by pressing gently. Trim any excess pastry if necessary.
6. **Brush with Egg Wash:** Place the wrapped Beef Wellington seam-side down on a baking sheet lined with parchment paper. Brush the entire surface with beaten egg, ensuring it's evenly coated.
7. **Bake:** Bake in the preheated oven for 30-35 minutes, or until the pastry is golden brown and the internal temperature of the beef reaches 130°F (54°C) for medium-rare or your desired doneness.
8. **Rest and Serve:** Remove from the oven and let the Beef Wellington rest for 10 minutes before slicing. Slice into thick portions and serve immediately.

Tips:

- Ensure the puff pastry is rolled out thin enough to cook through and become crisp.

- Let the Beef Wellington rest before slicing to allow the juices to redistribute.
- Serve with a side of roasted vegetables and a rich red wine sauce for a complete meal.

This Mushroom and Gruyere Stuffed Beef Wellington is an elegant dish perfect for special occasions or holiday dinners, combining tender beef with savory mushrooms and cheese wrapped in buttery puff pastry. Enjoy the luxurious flavors and impressive presentation of this classic recipe!

Pear and Gorgonzola Salad

Ingredients:

- 6 cups mixed salad greens (such as mesclun mix or baby spinach)
- 2 ripe pears, cored and thinly sliced
- 1/2 cup Gorgonzola cheese, crumbled
- 1/2 cup walnuts, toasted and roughly chopped
- 1/4 cup dried cranberries or pomegranate arils (optional, for sweetness)
- 1/4 cup extra virgin olive oil
- 2 tablespoons balsamic vinegar
- 1 tablespoon honey
- Salt and freshly ground black pepper, to taste

Instructions:

1. **Prepare Salad Greens:** In a large salad bowl, combine the mixed salad greens.
2. **Add Pears, Gorgonzola, and Walnuts:** Arrange the thinly sliced pears over the salad greens. Sprinkle crumbled Gorgonzola cheese and toasted walnuts (and dried cranberries or pomegranate arils if using) evenly over the salad.
3. **Make Dressing:** In a small bowl or jar, whisk together the extra virgin olive oil, balsamic vinegar, honey, salt, and black pepper until emulsified.
4. **Dress the Salad:** Drizzle the dressing over the salad ingredients. Toss gently to combine, ensuring the salad is evenly coated with the dressing.
5. **Serve:** Transfer the pear and Gorgonzola salad to serving plates or a salad bowl. Serve immediately as a refreshing and flavorful side dish or starter.

Tips:

- Choose ripe but firm pears for the salad to ensure they hold their shape and provide a crisp texture.
- Toast the walnuts in a dry skillet over medium heat for 5-7 minutes until fragrant, stirring frequently to prevent burning.
- Adjust the sweetness of the dressing by adding more or less honey to suit your taste preferences.

This Pear and Gorgonzola Salad is a delightful combination of sweet pears, tangy Gorgonzola cheese, crunchy walnuts, and a flavorful balsamic dressing. It's perfect for any occasion, from casual lunches to elegant dinners, offering a balance of textures and flavors that will please your taste buds. Enjoy the fresh and vibrant essence of this salad!